# WHAT PEOPLE [SAY ABOUT]
## *Love* BEYOND

"As a life coach, I work with singles and couples who want to move to a better place. As I read Christina's book, I recognized some common threads I teach and coach about. Good perspectives. God perspectives. While the goal of marriage is to point people toward God by serving your mate as Jesus served, these are great things to practice as a single person too.

"Christina will walk you through her journey, sharing what she learned along the way: Freely receive, and freely give. Take courage. Confront fear instead of being enslaved by it. Quoting the Bible along the way, she connects truth to her journey. I know Christina personally, and her Christian faith shines through with her words and actions. Enjoy *Love Beyond*! I did."

—ELIZABETH LEWIS
Life Coach, Relationship Coach, Author, and Speaker
www.loveandlaughterlifecoaching.com

"When my lovely friend Christina told me she was writing her story, I knew it would be two things—heartfelt and instructional. From her tender heart, she shares with her readers answers to some very painful questions. *Love Beyond* is a story of self-discovery and adventure written in Christina's signature storytelling style. This story of personal pain and triumph over difficulty will at times warm your heart or break your heart but will always leave you uplifted."

—BETTY THOMASON OWENS
Author of *Still Water: A Home Found Suspense*
and *Leave a Legacy of Love & Grace*

"It is an honor to endorse *Love Beyond: From Brokenness to Beloved*. I have known Christina for decades and watched her walk out the story she tells in this book. Over and over again, through the love and grace of God, she forgave her unfaithful husband. Most women would have left such a trying marriage—with good reason. I saw her stand in faith and turn the other cheek time after time. In *Love Beyond*, she shares the trials that beset her: rejection, betrayal, and unbearable grief. On countless nights, when her husband did not come home, she walked the floor, praying fervently, while tears flowed down her face, but she stood her ground and trusted Jesus through it all. He gave her strength. In our talks, she maintained faith, kept a sweet and Christ-like spirit, and pressed on. When the marriage finally ended, it wasn't her doing. She had done what she could.

"Any woman who is going through a difficult and disappointing marriage will benefit from her beautiful story. In the midst of Christina's 'dark night of the soul,' she encountered Jesus in a more personal and loving manner than she ever had before. He wiped away her tears, loved her tenderly, and healed her broken heart. The psalmist declared, 'He brought me up out of a horrible pit, out of the miry clay and set my feet upon a Rock. . . . He put a new song in my heart even praise unto God. Many shall see it and fear, and will trust in the Lord' (Psalm 40:2-3, paraphrase). *Love Beyond*, obviously inspired by the Holy Spirit, will bless everyone who reads it—no matter their situation in life."

—DIANA SCHEICH
Go Tell Ministries, Inc.

"This book, *Love Beyond*, is a beautiful example of listening and learning from God about His view of relationships. Christina describes her experiences in a vibrant, humorous, and straightforward way. Her writing is captivating and illustrates how one can go from surviving to thriving after a broken relationship. Her trust in God and His wisdom for her life have clearly led her to a life of joy and true fulfillment!"

—DEBRA BOBLITT
Former AAA Executive, Author, and Speaker

"*Love Beyond,* by Christina Sandrella, is a compelling story of God's unfailing love and empowerment of grace that gave her an unshakeable commitment to say yes! to God in otherwise impossible situations within her marriage. It reminds me of my nearly twenty-five-year commitment to my wife and the rollercoaster ride that it brings. If you don't want the ups and downs, then get off the rollercoaster!

"This book is a great read—an easy-to-understand outline of what it takes to make marriage work. By bringing in faith in God, she really reminds us of and incorporates many of life's what-I-learned-in-kindergarten concepts: Be kind to others. Don't lie. Be nice. Don't cheat. And many more.

"Christina is an incredible human being who has been in my life for a long time. I enjoy her enthusiasm for God and faith, her family, and her incredible passion for life. Truly inspirational!"

—WILLIAM E. SPAR
MA, CTP, LUTCF, Founder and Chief Tax
Strategist at ARP Tax & Estate Planning

# BEYOND

## FROM BROKENNESS TO BELOVED

## CHRISTINA FOTHERGILL SANDRELLA

KUDU PUBLISHING

*Dedication*

*To my three children, from the eldest to youngest, Randy, Anthony, and Mindy, I dedicate this book to you—the most important people in my life and my greatest joy!*

*Randy*
*Your wit and exuberance bring cheerfulness and laughter which are good like medicine. Your tender heart and strong arms have comforted me when life was not at all funny.*

*Anthony*
*Your logical perspective and opinions help keep me on track when my emotions sometimes run amok. Purposeful and determined as you are, I can always depend on you.*

*Mindy*
*You have extended great grace. Your compassion, understanding, and empathy have been a great encouragement and inspiration to me. You are Precious, my delightful daughter.*

*I can't imagine life without any one of you.*

*It is Love Beyond words!*

*Mom*

# CONTENTS

# FOREWORD BY TONY GORE

Some people have a story to tell, and some have a journey to share. Christina Sandrella has both.

Her story is a familiar one—recounting so many experiences, both good and bad, from her years following Christ as a godly woman of faith. Christina shares about heartache, rejection, and disappointment with a graceful sensitivity. She models for us a way of being that invites God into our pain.

Her journey is one that never loses sight of her truest Love—the Love of a Heavenly Father. And as she keeps her eye on Him, she invites us to walk with her, learning from Him and from her as we journey on.

It is indeed a rare person who has lived enough life to see both joy and pain and has the wisdom to find God in both. Christina does that in a way that welcomes us into the story God has allowed her to experience and then challenges us to do the same. Her journey from brokenness to beloved is one we should all feel fortunate she has chosen to share.

—TONY GORE
Founder and Director of Freedom Counseling Services

# FOREWORD BY MICHAEL HARMON

*Love Beyond* is not just a story, and not just a testimony, but it is the healing heart of the Father for those who are broken and who need to see His love manifest as wholeness.

Inside the pages of this book, you will see how the joy of the Lord changes the attitude of our hearts and will move us from a victim mindset to a victory lifestyle. Christina is filled with the joy of the Lord, as is her testimony. This book will set you on the path toward healing and the joy that follows us as we embrace God's plan of redemption.

Christina is authentic. She is a petite warrior for the Lord. When she speaks, she speaks from the purity of her spirit. When she writes, she writes from her healing and wholeness. When she ministers, she ministers from the very heart of God who has redeemed her from her own brokenness.

Through her ministry, and now her writing, Christina's life continues to touch others through the joy that emanates from her heart. Her laughter brings comfort and healing to all who will open their hearts to the Lord to receive the healing, the love, and the joy that this book offers.

*Love Beyond* will challenge you to experience God with the same contagious fervor and passion that has led Christina to love well and laugh often on her journey to wholeness.

As you read each chapter, you will get to know Christina personally, but more importantly, you will get to know the God of her testimony. She carries the glory of the Lord wherever she goes because she lives in His glory. You will see how her fierce spirit handles each situation by relying on the Lord to do battle for her. You will also see her ability to defeat every giant that attempts to stop her by trusting the God that lives within her.

Every word in *Love Beyond* is filled with the love and the joy of the Lord. Open this book and you will be drawn into an epic love story of a Father's love for His children and the restoration that comes from His healing nature.

—MICHAEL HARMON
Sr. Leader Community of Hope Church, Davenport, Iowa

# INTRODUCTION

I do not own my story. As His child, I've given Him the right to ownership—of my life. God is the author and finisher of this story. For quite a while, this book was on my mind, in my heart, and on the pages of my journal before I finally committed to just writing my story. Why the delay? My marriage was unpredictable, teetering on the brink of a breakup many times. I kept waiting, praying, and hoping for the last chapter to evolve the way I wanted, with a happy ending. You know, the way it should be—a godly marriage. The outcome, however, was unexpected and disappointing. Not a happy ending. Finally, I understood God already knows the end from the beginning, so I began writing. Because my marriage was on the rocks, the original title of the book was no longer suitable. So, I renamed it. If only it were that simple to fix what's broken in life.

The book is tinged with humor and light-heartedness; yet, it directly addresses personal matters that plague women such as loneliness, infidelity, identity crisis, unworthiness, and much more. Each page of my book has been written from my heart and not just my head. I felt like a little child, sitting on Daddy God's lap, and listening as He whispered the words to write. Father's arms were wrapped around me so tightly—it pushed all the ugly stuff out. In those intimate times, we sat together by the still waters, while cleansing streams of tears steadily flowed. In subdued anguish, I asked Him to help me re-experience heartfelt emotions as I wrote each chapter; therefore, tears are a welcomed companion of this book. Though they are not grief-stricken tears, there is sadness in knowing that divorce truly breaks God's heart and destroys what God loves—the family.

Who among us has not been hurt in a relationship? Such experiences often result in negative feelings about yourself that cause you to wonder if real love exists. Maybe you believe love is beyond your reach or has passed you by. I'm a young and vibrant seventy-three-years-of-age Christian woman still expecting and believing for remarriage—a godly marriage! Yet, I am content in where I am and who I am.

*Love Beyond* embraces the realization that love already exists and yet we spend a lifetime looking for it to be packaged in a particular way. You will discover that love is expressed in myriad ways. God is love (see 1 John 4:8), the source of perfect love. Jesus Christ came to reveal His Father's love and when we embrace Him, we become a conduit for love to flow in and through us. We can live from a place of already being loved perfectly, which can strip away layers of rejection, heal hurts of betrayal, bring joy in singleness, and provide contentment in our present situation.

Suppose there's been a glitch in your relationship and you're stuck because what you thought you knew fell apart, and there was no backup plan. It's a devastating and unwarranted experience. You begin doubting yourself and every decision—I could've, would've, should've syndrome brings confusion and guilt. When circumstances radically changed in my personal life and my marriage began faltering, I doubted if I should even write the book because the outcome was very different than expected. A bittersweet symphony describes my journey, yet the sweetness of God's presence enveloped me and far outweighed the distasteful bitterness of rejection and painful experiences.

Brokenness can sometimes lead to hopelessness. Its debilitating effects can embed itself in a heart desperately trying to hide or bury the pain. Although not visible to the naked eye, and when least suspected, its venomous fangs inflict pain and spew out lies of defamation of character. By depositing feelings of worthlessness, its evil intent is to create an identity crisis. There's no way to sugarcoat something so hideous as rejection.

My book gives insight into how to navigate through murky waters. Biblical principles, scriptural references, personal experiences, and learned lessons will foster a greater appreciation and understanding of God's extravagant love and power of His supernatural grace, which equips you to overcome every adversity—heartache, rejection, disappointment, insecurity—the list is endless. Having a different approach or perspective can be very helpful in hurtful situations. It's like looking through a different lens. For example, to abandon is to leave completely and finally; forsake utterly; desert. Unfortunately, this has occurred in far too many relationships and is not to be minimized. But let's put a different twist on its usual meaning. In a positive sense, abandonment is forgetting your past; it is leaving your future in God's hands and devoting the present fully and completely to Him.

The key is hearing the voice of God and, without hesitation, obeying Holy Spirit's guidance and instruction (even when you don't understand!). In doing so, you will be encouraged and find hope, which is the confident expectation of what God promised, and its strength is in His faithfulness. You can trust Him in every situation regardless of the outcome. Trusting God brings satisfaction to the present moment, in whatever that moment holds, because it contains God's eternal plan for you.

I believe LOVE is spelled T-I-M-E because that's how love grows. No substitute can compensate for the lack of it. Love gradually grows over time with roots that burrow deep into the soil of the heart. A key factor in nurturing love is through the expression of gratitude with such positive effects that help strengthen friendships and intimate relationships. Are you spending time with the One who loves you unconditionally? Is your heart overflowing with gratitude for Jesus' friendship?

Material possessions have no lasting value or influence. My story is a testimonial that will continue to impact you, the reader, long after the words have been read and after I'm gone. It is part of God's plan to bring freedom to you. I'm grateful for the opportunity to creatively express and share what I have discovered about His greatness and have experienced through the empowerment of supernatural grace and His enduring faithfulness. Hearing God's voice and being true to Him in word and deed is living life to the full each day.

God already knows the end from the beginning. The last chapter of my marriage wasn't a fairy tale happy ending to "live happily ever after." I didn't want my marriage to end at all; yet my life continues with resounding joy and the fulfillment of everlasting love. After the divorce, I went back to my roots—my maiden name, Sandrella—because it represents the blessing and richness of my Christian heritage. Furthermore, Sandrella sounds like Cinderella (as in the fairy tale). God really does make something beautiful out of ashes. It's *Love Beyond* your highest aspirations!

Today is a wonderful opportunity to love and to live for Jesus!

—Christina Fothergill Sandrella

# CHAPTER 1

# I DIDN'T KNOW WHAT I THOUGHT I KNEW

## *Love Beyond Your Mistakes*

*What is the purpose of love?*
*Is it merely for soul-satisfaction*
*To get what I desire*
*For attention and affection?*
*I would say, "Nay."*
*It's the giving away of self,*
*Like an arrow shot from a bow*
*That finds its way*
*into another's heart.*

**B**lissful wishing for an unrealistic fairy tale type relationship can falsely influence your expectations and decisions, resulting in making some royal mistakes in judgment and character. It can even delay the suitor if you're waiting for the perfect royal prince. So, you've made mistakes in relationships, who hasn't? You can still dream big but be realistic. And learn from your mistakes.

## THE PRINCESS YEARS: IF THE SHOE FITS, WEAR IT.

Being a princess is at the top of a little girl's dream list, so she becomes one on a grand scale in her own tiny imaginary world by adorning herself royally from head to toe. She dons a frilly princess gown with layers of tulle or satin, then accessorizes every visible part of her body with all that glitters and sparkles. This includes, of course, Mom's special gems. (This is when, after the "performance," a treasure hunt takes place to find all the missing items.) She crowns herself with a shiny tiara she places on her head before gingerly slipping her little feet into shoes with teeny heels. Thus adorned, courageously and regally, she prances around, stumbling periodically in her attempts at elegance. This behavior comes naturally.

At a very young age, she wants to get married—immediately—and knows who the suitor will be. Make no attempt to convince a princess of the possibility of her dream not coming true. It must! Where did such frivolous ideas originate? They're innate. Fanciful fairy tales, such as those about Cinderella and Rapunzel, fascinate and influence sweet, tender, and fragile hearts. Remember the magical kiss that turned a toad into a handsome prince? (Or maybe your experience was the opposite, and dreadfully worse—you kissed a prince who later turned into a toad!) Imagine, suddenly, on the horizon, a white horse appears, galloping furiously toward you, bearing a courageous knight who whisks you away into never-never land to rescue you from the monotony of life and the horrible ache of loneliness. An imaginary world can be so exciting!

Is it any wonder that in literature today, romance is one of the most popular genres? Pick up a romance novel authored by Nicholas Sparks (my favorite), Danielle Steel, or Nora Roberts that is compulsively readable, and it will make your head reel and your heart swoon. As you recline on the sofa at home, your imagination can take you to a faraway place full of excitement with thrills beyond your own experience. It makes you smile and inspires hope that love is surely on its way.

Although the head knows better than to believe in fairy tales, doesn't your heart still yearn for magical moments of love and romance in spite of disappointments, rejection, and heartbreaks? A healthy, loving relationship requires work and has nothing to do with your shoe size! Big foot. Little foot. It doesn't matter. What does matter is to have a big heart full of kindness.

What were your childhood dreams? What aspirations did you have? It helps to surround yourself with those who truly care about you and encourage you toward your dreams. In ninth grade, I knew I wanted to get married and be a stay-at-home mom. We're all different regarding what fulfills our desires.

Females exhibit strong innate tendencies toward sensitivity which are a beautiful part of who they are and how they've been uniquely designed. Learn to embrace the God-given traits of a compassionate, caring, and tender heart which is far more beautiful (and longer lasting) than makeup on a made-up face. Every woman is worthy of love. Many daughters reading this have experienced much pain and rejection within their own families where expectations were put upon them, and love was conditional based on their performance. As a child, perhaps, you weren't affirmed, and felt unloved, or your parents got a divorce and you felt abandoned.

Many years later when my daughter Mindy was well into her adult years, she and I had a mom-daughter-heart-to-heart talk. I was grieved to learn she had a deeply wounded heart—of feeling rejected because of expectations put on her, of believing love was based on her good performance, and there was much hurt about my divorce. I loved her always, unconditionally, but that was completely overshadowed at times because of conflict. Thank God, she was bold enough to tell me of her pain. When I heard her story and felt her pain, I felt guilty and ashamed. Through forgiveness, her wounded heart could be healed and our relationship could flourish as never before. Forgiving myself was very hard and humbling because of the lies hounding me of being an unworthy mom.

Every one of you is a daughter, and many of you are moms and even grandmothers. I pray that my story will give you hope and courage to open the door to reconciliation for you and your loved ones. Misunderstandings, disappointments, conflicts, and every conceivable hurt can be healed. Relationships can be restored through forgiveness and grace. God can reconcile the irreconcilable. He can reverse the curse. Love never fails.

## *Never sell yourself short. You have value.*

Never sell yourself short. You have value. Everyone has flaws and imperfections, but you are worth loving just as you are. God wants you to see yourself through His eyes and experience the reverence, awe, and majesty that went into making wonderful you. Cinderella's shoe doesn't need to fit you. There's a special pair made just for you to fit your walk perfectly to make the journey assigned to you. It could be a pair of hiking boots!

What captures the eye and ears often captures one's heart.

It can happen when least expected. Suddenly, someone takes your breath away! One look or a "Hello" is all it takes. Your brain turns to mush, and you feel like butterflies are doing somersaults in your stomach. It's hard to concentrate as you constantly dote on him. It's magical—a thrilling and hot sensation like a fireworks display glittering in the night sky. Maybe it lasts, or maybe the sparks eventually die out, but the momentary experience can happen at any age, in any place, and at any time. The memory can last a lifetime, even if a relationship never evolves. Who doesn't want the "fuzzy-wuzzy" indescribable feeling of love?

Heart-throbbing sensations? Love at first sight? A sentimental emotion that spontaneously erupts—but at the age of twelve? That's how young I was when I first saw Steve Fothergill at a Baptist church. He was fourteen when he caught my eye and attention, and he eventually captured my heart with his great sense of humor. It was no surprise that in his senior year, he was voted wittiest. He was cute, too! Naturally, at that young age, it was mere infatuation, but a strong attraction mushroomed quickly, and flirtation was high on my radar! Church was a perfect place for finding love, right? The wild roller coaster ride of emotions was exciting!

Females can sometimes maneuver things in order to get what they want, and I wanted to spend time with Steve as much as possible. Thankfully, various church-related socials and activities allowed us to be together at a young age. We played a lot of miniature golf, enjoyed ice cream socials, sang in the choir together, and then, at an appropriate age, we sat together during the service. Once he got his driver's license, my parents gave their consent for him to drive me home from church and social activities. Such was the slick path that soon led to dating when I was a teenager.

Quite the raconteur—Steve was a joker and a great storyteller. One of his favorite lines was, "Don't let the truth get in the way of a good story." Hindsight is insightful! There was truth in that very statement. Unfortunately, in defense of his vagrant actions outside the boundaries of marriage, he had a storyline that deviated from the truth. God sees and knows all things which are done in secret. There were times He gave me knowledge of what was going on, which I kept in my heart.

Plans that "they" made. Money that was being spent. It was important to have insight and information, but the greatest knowledge I received during that time was how to pray. Obviously, there was much I didn't know, nor will I ever know because there was no need.

Emotions are real, and females, characteristically, appear to be emotional by nature. Subconsciously and effortlessly, emotions are aroused that can influence your thinking and steer your actions, but they are not reliable. Emotions are to be controlled—instead of their controlling you. Learn to regulate the trigger and control the thermostat. Past experiences give opportunities to grow in wisdom and learn how to better bridle some of your wild and turbulent emotions. God's grace empowers you to live a self-controlled and godly life (see Titus 2:12).

A word to parents—be mindful of the possibility of your daughter or son meeting that special someone at a very early age and, in the future, having a potential son- or daughter-in-law. It happens. Get to know that person in more than a superficial way—look for more than what meets the eye! Regardless of the age of your child, you still have the opportunity to influence, and you always have the privilege to pray for them. As children become older, you are a coach—positioned to teach them rather than tell them what to do. You assist in helping them unlock their potential and demonstrate the values you want them to embrace through your own behavior.

## NO SUCH THING AS TIME

Have you ever been so caught up in love that you lost sense of everything else, especially time?

I was eighteen when time stood still. It was pure bliss: deeply breathing in ocean-filled air as the sound of subtle waves and the natural rhythms of nature were singing in my ears.[1] Standing beneath a host of stars glowing so brightly against a velvety dark sky, it seemed as though pockets of sunshine had been released for this very special

1 Baz Luhrmann, *Romeo and Juliet* (October 27, 1996; Burbank, CA: 20th Century Studios).

moment. I was ensconced in the arms of the love of my life. Completely enraptured in the most romantic atmosphere one could ever imagine or dream of. It was a surreal moment as Steve and I stood alone on the beach, talking about our future. Marriage. We had just seen the movie *Romeo and Juliet*. I was totally mesmerized.

## HEARING BUT NOT UNDERSTANDING

It's easy to misunderstand what's actually being said in conversation. You heard what was said and made a decision based on your perception that altered the course of your life. The dialogue reached a point where you are suddenly blaming each other:

"But you said . . . "

And the other party says, "But that's not what I meant."

Oftentimes, it's simply the difference between a male's brain and a female's brain. (Of course, women are always right—did I hear an "AMEN"?) Casual conversation, "small talk"—although it can be pleasant—requires little thinking because it lacks depth. Still, what you say or don't say is significant. Good communication is essential! A conversation can be the beginning of a deliriously wonderful foreseeable future with a person! Or, the piercing, anguished ending of a relationship or divorce. You need to know what your partner is actually saying. Recent research reveals ongoing communication difficulties are the number one reason couples divorce in the United States. According to one study conducted by the American Academy of Matrimonial Lawyers, 67.5 percent of marriages that ended did so primarily due to communication problems.[2]

---

2   Natalie Maximets, "What Makes Someone Ask for a Divorce," *Mediate.com*, 7 Nov. 2021, https://mediate.com/what-makes-someone-ask-for-a-divorce/.

*If you're not certain you understand what a person meant, ASK a question for clarification.*

If you're not certain you understand what a person meant, ASK a question for clarification. How often have you wondered what the other party meant by what they said and began analyzing it to death? Inevitably, you end up going down the rabbit hole. Undoubtedly, honesty is foremost in any conversation. When trust is developed, you can feel safe, and transparency becomes possible. Only one lie can cause mistrust.

## WHAT YOU DON'T KNOW COULD HURT YOU

Six years seems like a reasonable amount of time to get to know someone, wouldn't you agree? It's true that I was so young—just a child—and still thought as a child when Steve and I met and became childhood sweethearts. He was my regular Friday night date for years, but rarely did we go out on Saturday evenings. I thought it was because my curfew was earlier for going to church on Sunday mornings. What I didn't know and couldn't observe was Steve's lifestyle on Saturday nights. I didn't see the other side of him until after marriage. As we grew older and talked seriously about marriage, I thought I knew his character, personality quirks, behavioral patterns, peculiarities, and nuances. I was in love with the guy! And I married my childhood sweetheart.

## WHAT DIDN'T YOU TELL ME?

### A Lie Is Twisted Truth—Deception.

Problems arose early in our marriage. While fervently praying about our relationship, I recalled a vivid memory—the unforgettable romantic evening on the beach in Florida. It was regarding the significant conversation Steve and I had about getting married. This memory playback resonated loudly in my thoughts and in my mind, I could see his reactions.

Steve: "You don't want to marry me."

My response: "What do you mean?"

Steve: "You don't know me."

My response: "Of course, I do. I've known you since I was twelve."

That's all I could remember. There was the answer but it was vague, ambiguous, and deceptive, and I didn't understand what he was really saying. But Steve was right, I didn't know him. He omitted some very crucial facts about his character regarding sexual relationships, pornography, and alcohol consumption. Those were reasons I wouldn't have married him. But my emotions were leading me. All I thought and understood was that I loved this guy. He treated me with respect. Those four words, "You don't know me," blew away with the wind because my mind couldn't wrap around them. So, I dismissed what he said. It wasn't until after our marriage that I understood the underlying message as Holy Spirit revealed the truth to me.

## *Partial truth is complete deception.*

Before this conversation took place, I had known Steve for six years, from age twelve to eighteen. What he didn't tell me at the time would have absolutely influenced my decision. You can recognize the pattern. I was in love with him. I heard what he said but didn't understand. I didn't ask for clarification. Partial truth is complete deception. My emotions were more in control than my senses. I didn't know what I thought I knew. I thought he was a Christian. It was of utmost importance to me—a "must-have" in marriage. Instead, there were secrets in the dark that invaded our home and marriage.

## TRUE CHARACTER

Have you looked through rose-colored glasses or observed someone you really cared about only to discover the hypocrisy later? What you see may be appealing and resonate well with the soul, but it may not be genuine. Maybe this was your experience. You made a mistake, there were consequences, and you've lived with guilt. You're still plagued by hurtful experiences. Perhaps you waited for a very long time, hoping, praying, and believing that the one you loved would make the necessary changes and correct the mistakes to have a healthy, vibrant marriage. I believed in Steve more than he believed in himself because I knew God's transforming power could deliver him from his lifestyle. However, Steve chose his own path which led him further from God even as the chasm grew greater between us with our differing beliefs and opinions.

Without condoning wrong behavior, it's important to recognize and be thankful for the good even in a bad situation. Having an unfaithful husband was really bad; yet, undeniably, he possessed good and positive traits. In many ways he was very helpful as well as kind. He was diligent in his work and gained an excellent reputation as a pilot. There was never a reason to worry about finances, and generosity was an attribute of his. Steve helped with chores, did the grocery shopping while I cooked, and helped clean up after meals. We worked well as a team. He assumed the responsibility of car maintenance and yard work. I have three wonderful children—my greatest treasures—and my desire to be a homemaker was fulfilled. I'm grateful for all the positive things he did and for providing a good life for us.

In our latter years, after the kids were grown, Steve and I traveled extensively while living in Guam. We enjoyed great adventures and grand experiences—yet all I ever wanted was him—and for me to be the one and only true love of his life. NO THING could ever substitute real love. My marriage was unhealthy and very painful at times. The enemy's lies were that I was not good enough. Not smart enough. Not educated enough. Not interesting enough. It was a battle of the mind but it took me to my knees and I cried out to God. Even though I didn't *feel* loved or wanted, I would declare what He said about me. "I am beautiful. I am God's masterpiece. I am loved. I am held in the arms of God." I spoke Truth over the lies. I refused to be ensnared by resentment over Steve's wrong choices.

Although I unknowingly married a "church-goer," not a Christian, I felt I had disobeyed and failed God which brought guilt and condemnation. Then one day Holy Spirit reassured me I had not sinned. He knew my heart and motives and that I had not purposely gone against God's will. His unfathomable and divine grace brought healing and comfort. He set my heart free!

Ask God for wisdom in making all your decisions and choices (see James 1:5). He will navigate you through the uncertain and hurtful times in spite of yourself. If you have disregarded God's will, repent. He'll forgive and cleanse you of all your sins (see 1 John 1:9). Your slate is clean! Forgiven and free! God will strengthen you, help you, and uphold you. Whatever He asks of you, He will empower you to follow through and to stay the course.

Regret is something we tend to own but can't afford to keep. You did the best you could with the information you had. Mistakes don't define you.

## KEEP HOPING!

When my second-born son, Anthony, was nine years young, he was diagnosed with non-Hodgkin's lymphoma and was undergoing chemotherapy. One morning, while Anthony was in bed, he called to me, and I heard an urgency in his voice. I rushed in and as I leaned down to him, he pointed to a pile of hair on his pillow. Several clumps of hair had fallen out overnight. In his eyes, I could see pain, fear, and hurt; yet, he courageously said, "Mom, it's time to shave my head, BUT I'll be like

Samson in the Bible when my hair grows out because I'll be stronger than ever!" Then he said, "As long as I'm breathing, there's hope." (As I write this, Anthony is now forty-six years old.)

**You're still breathing!** You can have a living hope that allows you to believe and dream again. Steadfast hope that enables you to persevere and keep moving forward in life. My desire for you is this:

As Romans 15:13 says, may the God of HOPE fill you with all joy and peace as you trust in Him, so that you may overflow with hope through the power of the Holy Spirit (emphasis added).

**Forgive yourself for the mistakes you've made.** Guilt and shame have always been the enemy's game. They are his weapons to make you feel like a failure. Commit your failures to God, then confidently commit your future to Him and receive complete restoration through His abundant mercy and lovingkindness (see Psalm 86:13). The tender mercies of the Lord are new every morning! (see Lamentations 3:23). With His help you can have a better understanding of His plan and greater wisdom in your choices.

Open your heart, glean that which is good, and discard the bad. Anticipate the good that is already on its way, and know there is *Love Beyond* your mistakes.

# CHAPTER 2

# NEW TO EACH OTHER

## *Love Beyond Mediocrity*

> *"When you have had a taste of excellence,*
> *you cannot go back to mediocrity."*[3]
> —MAXIMILLIAN DEGENEREZ

## THE BEST DAY OF MY LIFE

I dreamt of the day that, as a bride, I would walk down the aisle of a church as the love of my life, Steve Fothergill, my husband-to-be, was eagerly awaiting the kiss that sealed the Marriage Covenant. The following was written in my journal as an expression of the emotion and overflow of love that I felt. . . .

> *To be young and intoxicated with love,*
> *Full of hope, wonder, and ecstasy.*

---

3  Maximillian Degenerez, "When you have had a taste of excellence, you cannot go back to mediocrity," *BrainyQuote,* https://www.brainyquote.com/quotes/maximillian_degenerez_636159.

*On my blissful wedding day—*
*'Twas the best day of my life.*
*As a blushing, radiant bride,*
*My rapturous heart burst with pride.*
*All I could do was smile,*
*As Father stood right by my side.*
*Enshrouded in a heavenly cloud,*
*I clung tightly to His arm*
*As we approached the sacred altar.*
*There, before God and man,*
*In our marriage vows, Steve and I covenanted,*
*To love and cherish each other always—*
*In good times and bad, in sickness and health.*
*Together we'd spend the rest of our days.*
*We hadn't many possessions or wealth;*
*Our greatest treasure was love for one another,*
*Which was more than enough.*

Love is intoxicating! Indescribable bliss! There's an adage that says "Ignorance is bliss," but it is not. When you're in a relationship, knowing the truth about that person is crucial. Integrity is invaluable for building trust and having a loving, healthy relationship. Unfortunately, our marriage, at best, went from bliss to a gradual but steady decline of mediocrity when I became aware of Steve's addiction to pornography which led to infidelity. Abuse of alcohol consumption further ravaged our relationship. When you don't honor yourself, you cannot honor the one you love. Mediocrity is just enough . . . but not deeply fulfilling or vibrant.

## NEWLYWEDS–HAPPY TOGETHER

A song by The Turtles titled "Happy Together" expresses an enthusiastic zest for the one you love and how every thought is wrapped around him day and night! That was me, at the beginning of our marriage, thinking about Steve and how happy I was when we were together. I wanted that for the rest of my life. My forever dream. La-La-land.

It was a fulfillment of the most dreamed of, hoped for, life-changing event, the best day of my life—my wedding day! Happy wife, happy life. Vows are made that are to last a lifetime. After marriage comes the baby carriage (if it's done God's way). You build a home (not a house). You make a life. As a happily married young couple, nothing seemed impossible.

As newlyweds, this glorious moment opened wide the door to a brand new life and new way of living in almost every way—extraordinary experiences and great adventures together, fresh and exhilarating, like inhaling the aromatic scent of a field strewn with lilies (my favorite flowers). Mmmm! Wonderfully blessed and blissful, I was now a newlywed.

## THE LOVE OF FAMILY

### The Sandrellas

*Like branches on a tree,*
*We all grow in different directions,*
*Yet our roots remain as one.*[4]

For me, marriage was the equivalent of expectations that looked like the loving family in which I grew up as a child. Having an Italian lineage, we embraced all the components of a large, vociferous, rambunctious family characterized by loyalty, love, and trustworthiness and demonstrated by strong hugs and robust laughter. The Sandrellas fit that description. Our household identified with the saying, "Love makes the world go round." God's love was the cohesiveness that kept us close together.

That's what I expected, hoped for, and carried into my own home to make it a safe place—God first with biblical principles to guide us, an

---

4   Suzy Kassem, *Rise Up and Salute the Sun* (Sedona, AZ: Awakened Press, 2011), 108.

abundance of love, lots of fun, but tempered with firm discipline. First would come marriage, next, the baby carriage. (That was the order in the Bible—marriage, then children.) My greatest desire was to have children and raise them in a happy, healthy environment. God fulfilled my dream to be a stay-at-home mom, and I lived a purpose-filled life.

## STABILITY OF MARRIAGE

A stable marriage can be likened to a three-legged stool—God, a husband, and a wife—all of which are necessary for stability in a marriage. If a stool is missing a leg, it will come up short! It cannot stand. In like manner, a marriage needs God. He truly is the stabilizing force. Without Him, it's unsteady and unreliable.

### The Three-Legged Stool of a Blessed Marriage: Selflessness, Forgiveness, and Communication

In an article by Dr. Michael Youssef,[5] he outlines three godly characteristics—selflessness, forgiveness, and communication—that are deemed essential to enjoy a blessed marriage. They cannot be minimized or ignored. A two-legged stool just doesn't work. Try to balance yourself sitting on a stool with only two legs—be prepared to pick yourself up off the floor! If one leg gets broken it has to be repaired to be sturdy. Marriage also needs to be strong and well-balanced. If one component of a blessed marriage is missing, it may not be visible like a broken leg of a stool, but it will likely break your marriage if you don't fix it. Do you want just a mediocre, unpredictable marriage or a great marriage that represents Christ and His beloved bride?

### Leg #1

We live in a "me" society. Selflessness, however, is the opposite of looking out for "number one." It isn't "tit-for-tat," "If you do this, I'll do

---

5    Dr. Michael Youseff, "The Three-Legged Stool of a Blessed Marriage," *oneplace*, accessed Feb. 9, 2024, https://www.oneplace.com/ministries/leading-the-way/read/articles/three-legged-stool-of-a-blessed-marriage-9210.html.

that." Nor does it keep a tally that puts conditions on love by tracking the "other's" lack of contribution. Instead, go ahead and be the one you want the other one to become. Keeping score wastes time and energy and robs you of seeing the good that's being done. The focus of selflessness is the "other" with a positive outcome as you manifest graciousness in consideration of the other person's needs, desires, opinions, and feelings. In a self-centered world, there's little evidence of this characteristic. Selflessness attracts love. Who wouldn't want to be thought of and appreciated in such an endearing way?

If you feel unappreciated and taken advantage of, how would you choose to respond? Or react? With vengeance? Resorting to hurtful, destructive ways and methods can only hurt you and will never resolve a problem. So, go the extra mile.

## Leg #2

Forgiveness should happen over and over again, as often as is necessary. ForGIVEness should never stop giving. Some things seem unforgivable because of the pain they've inflicted and without the grace of God, it may be impossible. Yet we are told to forgive one another and be kind and compassionate, just as Christ forgave you (see Ephesians 5:31-32). Hopefully, the same ill-begotten behavior won't be repeated but will be repented of. Try not to "sweat the small stuff" when it comes to irritating habits or annoying characteristics that really don't matter. Unforgiveness will keep you in bondage—forgiveness will set your soul free.

## Leg #3

Effective communication is the third leg and is crucial in any relationship. It's essential for a thriving intimate relationship as it allows couples to build trust, strengthen emotional intimacy, navigate conflict in a healthy and constructive way, and create a deeper understanding of each other. Even so, hectic schedules and tired minds and bodies can lead to weariness that wreaks havoc on communication. It's crazy, but important enough that you might have to schedule a time to talk without interruption. Set a date and time on the calendar. It's that important.

A girlfriend once shared that she and her husband had a nightly ritual before they retired. They'd sit on the edge of their bed and take at least fifteen minutes just to chat. She'd sip on her tea, and they'd engage in conversation. She said it was one of their most intimate times. If there had been a conflict, it was settled before they'd go to bed.

These principles are helpful in aspiring toward a great marriage and maintaining a well-balanced relationship that bears much good fruit. True success is keeping Christ at the center of your marriage. We often say "make time" for this or that and it's vital to make and take time to assess your relationship. If you want an honest answer and not just your own opinion about how you're doing, ask your spouse, "How am I doing in this area?" Listen with an open heart and hug each other after the conversation. Don't even think about sleeping in the other bedroom—rehearse and practice what you just learned!

The start of marriage and our new life together began as an adventure with our move to Florida—an expected transition since he was enlisted in the military at the US Coast Guard Air Station in Opa-Locka. Quite naturally, our married lives began as when we had first met—in church—as was our custom to attend regularly.

With a new identity came a different way of thinking since there was someone other than myself to consider (see Philippians 2:3). There was such excitement in this new life that it seemed dreamlike. I imagined it would encompass seasons of inexplicable wonder and astonishment, a new awareness of each other, surprising discoveries and pleasures, and aspiring dreams with hopes of success. Our children, and eventually grandkids, would be born, who would all contribute to life's most cherished and indelible memories to last a lifetime. Something untarnished. Fresh beginnings.

Pause a moment to recollect a moment in time, an incredulous event or occasion that made it the best day of your life! Take time to reflect on the unique feeling of that experience. Exuberance! Elation! Where you felt as if your heart would burst with enthusiasm! It's soul-refreshing to revisit such times that tremendously influenced you and even changed the course of your life. I choose to never forget the wondrous love and blissful, romantic times that led me to the altar in spite of the twists in life. Beginning life together as newlyweds was thrilling, exciting, somewhat mysterious, and wild!

Both Steve and I were in great health and quite active. Tennis, jogging, racquetball, walking, and hiking were part of our lifestyle. But staying at home was also enjoyable as we both liked to read, although we read different genres. There was pleasure in the mundane. I suppose there was nothing extraordinary about our routine, but love was the extraordinary part.

On the deep blue horizon was the hope of enlarging the family circle and celebrating special events and every conceivable holiday. Sure enough, the baby carriage came with Randy's arrival; thereafter, Anthony was born, and Mindy was adopted. In my eyes, children are worthy of the greatest celebration of all in this world. They are a gift and a reward from the Lord (see Psalm 127:3). Motherhood expands your heart and fills it with more love than you could ever imagine. It's about nurturing life. It's a huge responsibility and a great honor.

You are God's greatest treasure. There is nothing mediocre about you or God's love for you. Ask God to delve deep into your heart and uncover a buried treasure box. Jesus is the key. Unlock and open it. As you lift the lid, there's a mirror. You see the reflection of yourself. Gaze into it. Your search will reveal that you are the treasure, an invaluable gift. Created in God's image, you are fearfully and wonderfully made (see Psalm 139:14), and you are His masterpiece (see Ephesians 2:10). There's no one just like amazing you.

There are many different opinions about looking back at the past. Where there has been hurt or mediocrity in a relationship, sometimes we err when we "throw the baby out with the bathwater." It takes time and forgiveness to appreciate or extract anything good associated with a bad experience. However, it's important to sift through the heap of memories to learn lessons and to have gratitude for the good times. The main thing is to not harbor resentment and bitterness. You're the one who suffers in that situation.

> *"Though familiarity may not breed contempt,*
> *it takes off the edge of admiration."*[6]
> —WILLIAM HAZLITT

## FAMILIARITY

In a positive sense, familiarity is a relaxed friendliness where you're comfortable enough to give each other nicknames. It happens over time when the new becomes familiar and somewhat ordinary. Life has its ups and downs with undulations caused by inevitable, unexpected challenges. You try to just roll with the punches, keep looking at what's ahead, and move forward. However, when kindness and helpfulness are taken for granted and expectation replaces appreciation, the relationship wanes. What was once new and appreciated becomes familiar and gets overlooked. Because you've grown accustomed to it, you now expect it and lose sight of its value and importance. What was once new and regarded as being special is now all too familiar and customary. It's a subtle slippery slope downhill into mediocrity.

Soon, you begin to really learn about the other's quirks and peculiarities that cause you to question where they were hiding before you got married. You start noticing who says, "I love you," more often, who has to have the final word in a disagreement, and who's the first to apologize. You keep score. Then, there are the bigger annoyances like

---

6   William Hazlitt, *Delphi Collected Works of William Hazlitt (Illustrated)* (East Sussex, UK: Delphi Classics, 2015), 22.

having to put the toilet paper OVER the roll because he doesn't care or squeezing the toothpaste tube from the middle, not the bottom (which is the correct way, right?).

Wouldn't it be nice if marriage was always a party? But, of course, it isn't. Some people think it should be that way, so when the party's over, they split. Deep ravines and mountains that seem insurmountable are unavoidable. Life is laced with predictable seasons of rather dull and mundane experiences interspersed with ridiculous, hectic times where you don't even notice when you pass each other. You find yourself coming and going, somewhat in a daze, as you keep your nose to the grindstone. Communication dwindles and texting is hardly worth the time because it gets confusing and is insufficient. You lose true connection and become distant from each other as you grow further apart emotionally and physically, too exhausted and depleted of energy to notice or care. Soon, you become strangers in the night. Silence is welcomed as peace. You wonder what normal looks like and then question if it's worth the time and effort to recover what's been missing. The chasm becomes so great that you wonder if recovery is even possible. It's the scenario of a poor frog who would leap away from hot water but, if put into cooler water that is gradually warmed, won't respond in time to getting boiled. As a metaphor, it speaks of gradual change where you may not be happy where you end up, but you didn't notice how you got there. No family is exempt from crises or heartache at different junctures in life, yet the glue that can bind a couple and family together is an active, living faith in God. Putting prayer as the foundation of your home will sustain you. Let Jesus be the Cornerstone.

One unforeseeable crisis in our family was when our son, Anthony, at nine years of age, was diagnosed with non-Hodgkins lymphoma. Nothing can prepare a parent for such horrendous news. A nurse commented on how common it was for a couple to separate and divorce when a child gets cancer because of the tremendous stress it puts on a marriage. Yet together, we made it through such an incredibly tough period—not just once—but twice when the cancer returned with a vengeance following a year of remission. Life was again turned upside-down. Anthony then underwent a bone marrow transplant. Even so, God performed a miracle as Randy's DNA was the perfect match and he was the bone marrow donor for his brother. I'll never forget how glad Randy was to be "chosen" and even in his pain the next morning, he said, "I'd do it all over again." In great sorrow, God brought great joy.

Although Steve and I dealt with the painful circumstances differently, our focus was Anthony and working toward getting him well again. We worked together to see him through the dark valley of the shadow of death to live and enjoy life again as every child deserves.

## HAPPINESS IS RELATIVE

Relatively speaking, I wish happiness always lived in our home. It did not. To believe marriage will be the source of your happiness is a delusion that can only lead to disappointment. Though happiness is not the goal in marriage, you can and should be happy in your marriage. You chose your mate! And within marriage, the choices and decisions one makes ought to contribute to more happiness than sorrow. With two lives completely thrown together in every aspect (financial, creative, career/job, sexual, and more), anticipate differences of opinion which can actually complement the relationship rather than cause conflict and hurtful confrontations. If your personal happiness is paramount, you'll be tempted to blame anything that impedes it on the other person. *That,* in itself, is a big problem.

God's greatest purpose for creating marriage is to show the world an earthly representation of what Christ's covenant relationship looks like with His Church. A few basic fundamentals of a strong marriage have been emphasized in this chapter. Qualities of unconditional love, respect, and honor, with both husband and wife fully surrendered to Jesus Christ, will cause your relationship to flourish. Yet, our culture's representation of marriage is poorly patched together from personal unhealthy experiences and past trauma that do not reflect a godly, wholesome perspective. I longed for our marriage to be a spectacular union because it was created by God Himself. Approaching marriage with a selfless heart and gospel lens is the key to building a beautiful, Christ-exalting relationship.

Our marriage was fundamentally broken because the foundation was unstable. Feelings are frivolous and unreliable. They can change with the wind. The feeling you had when you first married isn't always going to be present, but you just stick with it. Commitment requires diligence and perseverance that will allow you not only to survive but to excel and thrive in your relationship. Let your roots grow deep in Christ and your heart be fertile soil where God's Word will establish and sustain you. May your passion for Him overflow into your marriage relationship. Marriage is both wonderful and challenging. "Two are better than one, for they can help each other succeed. If one person falls, the other can reach out and help" (Ecclesiastes 4:9-10, NLT).

I envisioned growing older with my husband and walking hand-in-hand (sometimes to literally help hold each other up!) while keeping in step with one another, or until that last goodbye kiss when our love slipped away into eternity. *Love Beyond* mediocrity is to love one another as Christ loves you. Unconditionally, always, and forever.

# CHAPTER 3

# LANGUISHING LOVE

## *Love Beyond Reason*

WITHERING LOVE
*"The petals are falling one by one*
*From the first rose you bought me*
*I had it freeze dried so it would last forever*
*Forever turned out to be much shorter than expected. . . ."[7]*
—VICTORIA HART, AUG 2013

Trust is gained when others can depend on you to do what you say you will. Your actions inevitably communicate your true love quotient. It seems nonsensical to remain in a marriage where there's no guarantee of fidelity or faithfulness. However, experiencing God's unfathomable love enabled me to love Steve beyond reason.

---

7    Victoria Hart, "Withering Love," All Poetry, Aug 2013, https://allpoetry.com/poem/10846271-Withering-love.-by-Victoria-Hart.

God is not the cause of your pain; He is your companion in pain and healer of your pain.

## IT ISN'T AS IT APPEARS

Steve and I were as much in love as any newlywed couple could have been. Like a fountain springing up, symbolizing life and purification, our love was genuine, fresh, and exuberant! Pure, untainted love springing forth from pure hearts. (Or so I thought.) There were no hurdles to jump over and no uncertainty about our decision to get married. Thoughts, concerns, or fears about extra baggage or skeletons lurking in the closet never crossed my mind. Ignorance was bliss. With few material possessions to begin our life together, we were rich with an abundance of love, and everything else was secondary. Moving to Florida where Steve was stationed at the US Coast Guard air station at Opa Locka was an exciting start! Life was sweet.

## ITALY–UPSIDE AND DOWNSIDE

"Do you want to move to Italy?" Seriously? What a surprising and fabulous question. That's the land of my heritage. "Yes! When do we leave?" I was ready to pack my bags. An opportunity of a lifetime presented itself for a three-year *hardship* tour in Naples—somebody had to do it. I knew life was going to be an adventure!

Italy was absolutely beautiful and, oh, so very romantic. Unfortunately, it actually turned out to be a hardship tour—hard on our marriage. It was absolutely a dream come true—and a nightmare all at the same time. There were many amazing and wonderful experiences, like being on a high, but the low places diminished much of the joy and excitement. Wine was cheap and soon, a pattern of excessive drinking became evident in Steve.

Far from family, in a foreign land, I was confused, disappointed, and hurt by the conflict his drinking created. Not knowing what to do, but certainly praying, God saw my sorrow. In a most unlikely and unexpected way, He rescued me. The air station closed, and our tour was shortened to nine months, which was a good thing. Young and confused about this demon of alcoholism, I had mixed emotions. There was disappointment in having to leave because there was so much more to explore, yet, I was relieved to return to the States and be closer to home. Unfortunately, drinking continued to escalate, which plagued our relationship. Excessive drinking and infidelity coupled up.

The Lord was with me and helped me (see Isaiah 41:10). Are you in a place that feels foreign to you? It doesn't have to be geographical. It can be a place of uncertainty and fear. You feel discombobulated! He will come to your aid when you feel helpless. Pray and seek God because He specializes in things you wouldn't have thought impossible.

## LOVE'S VERY NATURE IS VOLUNTARY

Volunteering is an honorable and selfless act of kindness and generosity. True, unadulterated love, in any relationship, is voluntary. A choice. A gift—you don't owe anything. Yet, to love another is costly since it involves sacrifice. You can't make someone love you nor should you try and earn it. Picture your hand wide open, filled with sand. It stays right there until the moment you try to hold on to it and close your hand. The tighter you make a fist to hold on to it, the more it trickles through your fingers until only a few grains of sand remain. Love was slipping through my fingers. I was working hard at wanting to be loved. To be noticed.

*Love can exist if it is not returned, but it cannot sing until it is shared.*[8]

Have you been with someone who was merely going through the motions of love, performing perfunctory obligations? It was all too obvious the heart was roaming elsewhere, and the emotions were on vacation. Present in the body but the soul was far-removed. Genuine love is not for self-gratification, which is a gross assault against another.

---

8   Chaim & Laura, "Word Study: Love (Chav, Racham), *Chaim Bentorah Biblical Hebrew Studies*, 9 Dec. 2016, https://www.chaimbentorah.com/2016/12/word-study-love-2/.

Nor is engaging in sexual activity necessarily a loving experience. (God's way is sex only within the marriage covenant.) When love is given, its fulfillment and completion come when love is received and returned.

## A WITHERED HEART

To wither is to become weaker or smaller and eventually disappear, to lose importance, to decline, and to fade. As a beautiful, fragrant bouquet of flowers eventually withers, becomes brittle and dies, a once thriving and vibrant relationship can decline when a withered heart loses its vitality and zest.

Typically, there are warning signs when bickering, sarcasm, a lack of appreciation, or apathy become the norm as acceptable behavior even though it feels unpleasant and results in irritations and aggravations. Or it could be that silence becomes more common (and preferred) rather than talking and laughing. Your love bouquet may have a few beautiful blooms and look okay, but the relationship stops growing, decays, and eventually dies. Healthy relationships need lots of nurturing.

While the marriage was sadly withering and love was languishing, my relationship with Jesus grew more intimate. His Word nourished my soul. His truth sustained me. He was the lily in the valley. Apart from Him, I would have given up.

## COMMUNICATING LOVE

Ralph Waldo Emerson said, "Thought is the blossom; language the bud, action the fruit behind it."[9] In humility, we value others above ourselves (see Philippians 2:3) and consider their welfare above ours. Real love genuinely wants to please the one you love and sincerely derives pleasure in doing so. It's contrary to the idea that many conditions have to be met before love is given. Guarding your heart can help set healthy boundaries. However, when you've been hurt, there can be a tendency

---

9   Ralph Waldo Emerson, "Thought is the blossom; language the bud, action the fruit behind it," *QuoteFancy,* https://quotefancy.com/quote/893496/Ralph-Waldo-Emerson-Thought-is-the-blossom-language-the-bud-action-the-fruit-behind-it.

to overreact out of fear and set up protective walls that will not serve you well. Walls may keep bad people out, but they can also keep good people out who could enrich your life.

Communication is the foundation of a healthy relationship. Talk to each other—as often as necessary. This depends on the two of you. I strongly suggest praying *with* each other often, especially prior to engaging in a serious conversation. Share what's really on your mind. Speak soon and honestly when you have a problem to avoid letting emotions fester. Discuss the uncomfortable issues. Pick your battles, but don't sweep things under the rug. You shouldn't be afraid to discuss any subject—fear itself is a sign of trouble. Take the initiative to contribute to your relationship with tangible acts of service. Let each other know your personal love language—words of affirmation, quality time, gifts, acts of service, and physical touching. (In *The 5 Love Languages*, Gary Chapman discusses this subject.)[10] Sow seeds of kindness to show you care about the other person. It will build character and positively benefit you in any relationship going forward.

## SUBSTITUTIONARY GIFTS

Money can't buy happiness—and money can't buy love. Buying gifts is no substitute for affection. It's not a fair exchange, especially when it's given to help ease a guilty conscience because of one's behavior. It's humiliating. Many gifts that Steve bought me had a motive behind them.

Some of those gifts were very nice but self-serving: a piano kept me occupied while he kept busy in other private ways; buying me a personal laptop gave him his laptop for "personal" reasons; he lavished me with flowers. On our last anniversary (our 42nd), his gift was quite grand—a new car—which turned out to be the goodbye gift. He left a few months later. She got him; I got the car. Stuff! All I wanted was all of him.

---

10 Gary Chapman, *The 5 Love Languages: The Secret to Love that Lasts* (Chicago, IL: Northfield Publishing, 2015).

A verse that comes to mind is 1 Samuel 15:22 (NLT): "Obedience is better than sacrifice." Isn't that sometimes what we do to appease God? Offer Him our talents, gifts, time, or money when, instead, all He wants is our love and worship?

## "O BE CAREFUL LITTLE EYES"

*O be careful little eyes what you see,*
*For the Father up above*
*Is looking down in love.*[11]

That little rhyme was taught in Sunday School when I was very young, but it isn't just for little children any longer. The vices of pornography and alcohol ravished our relationship. We never made it to the seven-year itch—the typical year said to make it or break it for marriages—a feeling of restlessness or dissatisfaction in a marriage.

## ROAMING HEART AND WANDERING EYES

Our first separation occurred in less than five years of marriage when life came to a screeching halt. I knew we had problems but when Steve announced he no longer wanted to be married and was moving out, that thought never crossed my mind. Mangled emotions threw me into an abrupt tailspin. I'd be left alone in North Carolina with our son Randy who was just nine months young. Marital distress was an intense difficulty and I was devastated. No longer was there any believable sincerity of Steve's wedding vows as there was no longer any credibility. He was in an extramarital relationship . . . one of several. Was I just another *one*—except that we were married? Here are my thoughts from a journey entry. . . .

*Two's company, three's a crowd.*
*In marriage, it's especially true.*

---

11 Cedarmont Kids, vocalists, "O Be Careful, Little Eyes," 1995, track 9 on *Action Bible Songs*, Zondervan Music Publishers.

*When you've said, "I do,"*
*Then do what you say.*
*Marriage is neither a game,*
*Nor a time to play.*
*You can love only one,*
*So put the other one away.*
*It's a new day.*

There was no Plan B because I never imagined my marriage falling apart. Choosing not to remain in North Carolina alone, I went to Louisville. Where could I go but home to my parents and figure out "what next?" It was such a hard place to be but that's where I was loved and surrounded by prayerful family, such a different environment than in my own home where I felt unwanted and unloved by my husband. Not once did they ever utter a harsh or unkind word about Steve, and I know their hearts were broken. Instead of judgment, they prayed for him *and* encouraged me to do so. I learned so much about unconditional love from them. This is where the really difficult part of my story began.

Have you been in such a broken place you couldn't think straight? You felt like your heart was going to burst and it was difficult to breathe. My family embraced me lovingly and had compassion even toward Steve. Maybe you're hurting right now and have no one to truly help you through the pain. It was God who held my broken heart and gave me strength and hope. He was the One who watched over me while I slept and never left me at any waking moment. He'll never forsake you (see Deuteronomy 31:8).

Because Louisville had so many memories, I said "yes" to my sister Claudia's invitation for Randy and me to stay with her and Charlie in Michigan for an indeterminate time. I felt like a bird with a broken wing that couldn't fly. I was alive but could only limp. Although my future was uncertain, my hope in Christ was the anchor for my soul (see Hebrews 6:19). In the midst of a raging tempest and tumultuous storm, I felt secure because of my personal relationship with Christ. He was my lifeline.

Have you ever been displaced? Like you're between a rock and a hard place? A song by Brooke Ligertwood titled "Honey in The Rock" exemplifies a picture of God's sweet goodness in places we don't expect to find it. The song references Psalm 89 where the Lord fed the Israelites with honey from the rock. Even in the barrenness of your life, you can still experience the sweetness of Jesus and trust Him. In my brokenness, I, and my baby boy, Randy, were profoundly loved and provided for by Claudia and Charlie. I was grateful for peace in the chaos.

It was several months later that Steve eventually responded to my call. I was dumbfounded when he blurted out the question, "Do you want the marriage?" Without an apology. Without any discussion about the separation. With no time to ponder the question, I had to make a decision that would affect the course of my life and my son's. It was tough. Thoughts and questions came rushing into my mind like a flood. The pain of rejection was deep but I wanted what God wanted. Divorce breaks His heart. Steve and I had a child, and I still loved my husband. The verse in Matthew 19:9 references adultery as a legitimate reason for divorce. But what about 1 Corinthians 7:13—when a Christian woman has a husband who is not a believer but is willing to live with her? Should she not remain with him? This was my current situation and the Bible had something to say about it. Would I opt for divorce? Or would I consider the *higher law of love and total forgiveness to open the door for reconciliation?* My response was, "Yes, I want the marriage." Conditions were put upon the reconciliation as Steve said he'd never go to church again and I was never to ask him. My response was, "I will continue to go to church and will take Randy with me." Thus, we reunited in marriage but we were coming apart. A "house divided against itself will not stand" (Matthew 12:25, NKJV).

God was pursuing Steve and I knew that to be true. That's *why* I remained in covenant marriage—as a God-given assignment. Although the future was unpredictable, the key was in knowing God's will in the moment, abiding in, and communing with Him in my daily walk, and saying "yes" in obedience to Him. I could trust God's plan because all the ways of the Lord are loving and faithful for those who follow the ways of His covenant (see Psalm 25:10).

I hoped that infidelity would never occur again. That was not the case. However, I could stand upon the promises of God. He was with me; He strengthened me; His grace was sufficient in every situation; in His presence there was still joy; He's the healer of broken hearts. I kept God's Word close to my heart, believed, and declared what He said. That's what helped me to be steadfast and kept me from never giving up.

With every heartbreak of infidelity, I went before the Lord to inquire of Him. My question was always the same, "What now, God?" I had to decide whether to stay or leave. I needed to know His will in each circumstance, and He answered every time I called on Him. The answer was always the same—"*If Steve wants to reconcile, be reconciled.*" That's *how* I knew I was to remain in the marriage. Over time I asked, "What is the purpose, God?" His response humbled me in a most profound way that forever changed my perspective and heart. It really wasn't about me. It was about a loving heavenly Father pursuing Steve. And I was chosen and trusted to be the conduit through which the love of Jesus Christ could flow and be revealed. I saw Steve through God's eyes. Once I was lost in need of a Savior—and Jesus loved me while I was yet a sinner. In like manner, I was to love Steve unconditionally even as an unfaithful husband.

I was not a victim. It was a choice that could only be accomplished through the power of God's supernatural grace and immeasurable love that saturated my heart in astounding ways and empowered me to love unnaturally. I, myself, do not possess such love; it is Christ in me. Neither would I, nor could I, grant such unfathomable forgiveness as was necessary. Many friends said, "God wants you happy. You don't need to stay in the marriage." Or they'd insist I hadn't heard right.

Their intentions were meant for my good because they didn't want me hurting. But they were wrong! The Bible assures me that obedience is what God requires, and He blesses the one who obeys; He proved that to be so in many remarkable ways which may seem like an anomaly. In my weakness, He was infinitely stronger! (see 2 Corinthians 12:10).

Of course, there was pain and an ocean of tears in the process. There were grueling times when I could only utter moaning and groaning from pain of rejection, but Jesus understands unintelligible words of the heart and can read tears. The Lord kept me from suspicion and jealousy, otherwise, I could never have remained in the marriage. I would've died on the inside. Yet, how can that be? Just put it in the category of imponderables and the inexplicable. The miraculous. I was not a martyr but a faithful wife, a believer in and worshiper of an Almighty God and Heavenly Father. The Creator of everything. Could He not create in me a way to love that's beyond reason? Steve was good to me. He had a sin problem and like every one of us, he needed Jesus.

What assignment have you been given that's beyond your human ability and limitations? Who do you need to forgive? Or, perhaps, ask for forgiveness from another? Although it's hard to do and very humbling, it's more rewarding than you can imagine. Who can you go to and say, "I love you" in spite of it not being reciprocated? God will lift you up! Obedience leads to blessings for you and others. It's essential in cultivating personal growth and demonstrates genuine love for God. He works in you to do His good pleasure (see Philippians 2:13). Seek God. Submit your will and watch Him work wonders in your life.

Christ's sacrificial love is in pursuit of each person. Have you accepted the greatest of all gifts—eternal life? "For God so loved the world, that He gave His only Son, that whoever believes in Him should not perish but have eternal life" (John 3:16, ESV). You, too, can experience God's supernatural *Love Beyond* reason and thrive in amazing ways.

# CHAPTER 4

# BITTERSWEET SYMPHONY

## *Love Beyond the Music*

*Music is a moral law;*
*It gives a soul to the universe,*
*Wings to the mind,*
*Flight to the imagination,*
*And charm and gaiety*
*To life and to everything.*[12]
—PLATO

**C**an you imagine how dull and sullen, bland and colorless, life would be without music? Music has been my close companion and has greatly influenced every season of my life, from early childhood

---

12 Plato, "Music is a moral law. It gives soul to the universe, wings to the mind, flight to the imagination, and charm and gaiety to life and to everything," *BrainyQuote*, https://www.brainyquote.com/quotes/plato_109438.

with happy songs, into the later melancholy seasons of my soul. The soul connects with music in a universal language that reaches everyone, expresses the inexpressible, and speaks where words fail while creating lingering memories—often, for a lifetime. Couples usually find their own unique songs that become very special and personal to their relationship.

It's no surprise that romance is at the top of the list. Particular songs still trigger emotions that tend to take me to places I don't want to go because they link to moments of the past. Coffee and a good read make me happy, and I like exploring different coffee venues where music is always playing. On occasion, a particular familiar ballad would play, and all I could do was snivel as I sipped my coffee. Does that ring a bell for you? You're caught by surprise at a vulnerable moment because your song came on and took you strolling down memory lane?

*Music has a way of getting to you, in you, and through you all the way to the bones!*

For creatures of extreme emotions with great pendulum-like mood swings, music possesses the powerfully persuasive ability to influence us in tremendously fascinating ways. An entire gamut of dramatic feelings—both positive and negative—are aroused: great joy, exuberance, beauty, sadness, relaxation, excitement, romanticism, passion, sentimentality, and even anxiety. Every conceivable emotion. Music has a way of getting to you, in you, and through you all the way to the bones! Its frenzied effects can make you quiver, shudder, and shiver and cause the hairs on your arms to stand on end. With its fascinating, inspiring, and transforming powers, it's simply magical. In the words of jazz great Louis Armstrong, "Music is life itself."[13]

Celebratory songs of joy and frivolity, dirges—melancholic with deep sorrow and grief, melodious and harmonious sounds or cacophonous and mournful sounds are all experienced in a symphony that resonates with life itself. In the sweet beginning of marriage, sunshiny days were abundant (literally because we lived in Florida), and music filled the air! As teenagers, Steve and I sang in the church choir. When married, I'd listen for him whistling a tune as he walked from the car to our front door. A song was on his lips and in his heart, always a happy melody, a happy tune. I don't remember when the whistling stopped.

As a couple, we had our favorite songs as well as our own. Over time, however, I realized some of his favorites were songs from other relationships. Their favorites. Many things of which I became aware were never mentioned. Entombed secrets. When growing up, Christian music played throughout the day at home. Never had I thought that would become an issue in my home, but it became a point of conflict. If Christian music were playing, Steve would exit the living room and go elsewhere, most of the time without saying a word, yet his actions were loud and clear. As much as possible, I wanted peace (see Romans 12:18), so I rarely played it. Privately, though, I listened to my music, though my happiness tinged with sadness.

A bittersweet symphony seemed to describe how I perceived my marriage. A simple definition and brief illustration of a symphony is that it's a lengthy form of musical composition or harmony of sounds or colors that has four movements—like chapters in a book. On the surface, our marriage appeared to have harmony, but there was so much dissonance and disagreement regarding integrity and commitment. There wasn't yelling or bickering, but it was inharmonious, and the vibrations weren't good.

---

13  Louis Armstrong, "Music is life itself," *Elevate Society*, https://elevatesociety.com/music-is-life-itself-what/.

Within a symphony, the first movement (called a sonata) is often the most significant. That's also true of marriage; how you begin and the foundation you lay are extremely important. The second is usually slow and lyrical. I suppose this was the movement of learning about each other in a much deeper way rather than just what met the eye. It was also more than hearing what the other person said—it was observing. The third movement in a symphonic composition is usually a dance. Dancing wasn't part of our lifestyle, but we sure danced to a lot of tunes in the many times of moving and transitions due to his career as a pilot, and during the years of raising our children there was a song and a dance! After raising our family, traveling was the dance of life that spawned gaiety and frivolity. Yet, contrary to the way things appeared in the prevailing atmosphere, there was an undercurrent of marital problems with secrets concealed in the dark. The ending, or fourth movement, is a prolonged final sequence—the finale.

Then the applause comes, and the curtain is drawn. Our declining marital relationship was definitely prolonged and painful—the finale was bitter, not at all sweet. When the curtain closed, there was no standing ovation. If the four movements of a symphony are like chapters in a book, I am now writing the book after the four movements in our marriage, at the finale. It was time to face the music: Steve was not willing to get help with his addictions. Bittersweet experiences are part of life, but bitter should not become the predominant taste.

> *Bittersweet experiences are part of life, but bitter should not become the predominant taste.*

You've likely been hurt at some juncture in life, caught off guard, and faced with overwhelming challenges. What do you do in those times? While growing up as a child, we prayed about everything, which was a lifestyle, and I did the same in my marriage. Although women typically find it easy to talk about personal problems, gossiping only adds fuel to the fire. Continually rehearsing a problem, especially concerning a personal relationship, only exacerbates the problem because it causes outrage to rise. Be certain your motive is pure when sharing your hurts with another. In choosing godly women who are trustworthy, we do not have to walk alone during difficult seasons in life. A true friend will walk alongside you, to love you, lift you up, and encourage and support you through all the twists and turns of life (see Proverbs 17:17 and 1 Thessalonians 5:11). And she will tell you the truth even if it hurts.

## MUSIC TO MY EARS–THE CRESCENDO

The sweetest sound on earth is the crying of a newborn baby. Heavenly music! Our children's growing up years had their own amazing cacophony of blessings and trials. Our firstborn spunky son, Randy, was born September 12, 1974, in Corpus Christi, Texas. Wow! I was a mom! On November 22, 1976, in Kodiak, Alaska, I gave birth to my second son, good-natured Anthony. Nothing compares with such exuberance as your baby's birth or adoption. From 1980-1985, we lived on the island of Oahu, Hawaii, where Steve was stationed in the Coast Guard for five years. During that time, Mindy, who was born on May 18, 1980, in Seoul, Korea, became our daughter on August 23, 1983, through adoption.

## THE BITTER AND THE SWEET!

Either imagine a beautiful place you'd like to visit or flip through the album pages of your mind and recall a place that has special memories. Hawaii was on my list—R&R (relaxation and romance, in spite of the fact that we had two small children!). There were great expectations of thrilling opportunities and forthcoming adventures. It was sweet, but it was mixed with bitter disappointment as infidelity continued to rear its ugly head.

As a result, Steve had moved out of our home and moved in with a mutual friend, John. Divorce proceedings were in progress and about to be finalized as Christmas approached—a most terrible time of the year to have to go through a divorce. It was going to be a really tough holiday season, so I made plans to go home to Louisville with the boys to "figure out my life."

I'm about to share a very personal story because of its impact on my life and, hopefully, you might see the lesson. This is a matter I have never mentioned to Steve. As I planned and packed, God impressed upon my heart that I was to meet with "her"—the woman with whom Steve was having an affair—the person who was wrecking my marriage. I knew her personally, sort of a family "friend" (as I shake my head . . . ). I wrestled with and resisted the thought of meeting her and tried to ignore the still small voice of God. Finally, I relented and called her, hoping she wouldn't answer, but if she did, I was sure she wouldn't meet with me! To my surprise, she agreed to meet at the McDonald's parking lot. I had no idea what I was going to say. This was strictly an act of obedience to God.

I prayed earnestly beforehand, asking God, "What in heaven's name am I to say?" There was no script. When I pulled into the parking lot, she came and sat in my car and a forty-minute conversation followed. It was a civil, earnest, honest, and forthright talk. I shared events about Steve and our relationship—the upside and the downside, how very much in love we were at one time, his positive and good characteristics, and those character flaws that crushed our marriage due to his infidelity and drinking. Ultimately, the conversation turned to God as I knew there was purpose, and it wasn't about my hurt or pain. I said I forgave her—it took her by surprise, and she tried to convince herself, and me, that the relationship she and Steve had was okay because they loved each other. I felt a sincere love for her and got to share with her the salvation message and tell her about the love of Jesus. She responded by saying she was Catholic; however, there was no understanding of a personal relationship with God. I gave her the opportunity and invitation to accept Jesus as her Savior. Although reluctant to do so right then, she now knew the truth. I'll never forget that moment.

As planned, I went to Louisville which was a gift from God. I needed love! And my family filled that longing. Christmas was a blur, but I clearly remember my brother Jon stepping up and into my boys' lives while we were there. He romped and wrestled with them, played with them, tickled them, teased them, and had them giggling. They had so much fun with Uncle Jon. He filled the gap, making life happy for them at such a confusing and difficult time for little boys and took a burden off my shoulders. He was there for my boys, and I was home with my family, which was the best possible scenario. During this time, I decided my life as a single mom would begin at my parents' home and from there, only God knew.

## THE DIRGE

John Paul Friedrich Richter said, "Music is the moonlight in the gloomy night of life,"[14] and I concur. Sometimes there are no second chances.

The night the boys and I returned to Hawaii, Steve was to pick us up at the airport so he could see the boys. He wasn't there. Instead, his friend John met me. As we walked to the car, he asked if I wanted to know why Steve hadn't come to the airport. My response was curt: "No, it really doesn't matter. I stopped believing him a long time ago."

John insisted and took hold of my arm to stop me. "You need to know why because 'she' crashed in the side of a mountain this morning. She's dead." (She was a helicopter pilot.)

My head was reeling. All I could say was, "Oh, God! Dear God!"

John continued to tell me the unstable condition Steve was in—outrageous anger against God. What a shame that God is so often wrongly

---

14 Jean Paul Friedrich Richter, "Music is the moonlight in the gloomy night of life," *LibQuotes, https:// libquotes.com/jean-paul/quote/lba1p2x.*

accused and blamed for bad things, yet seldom acknowledged for all the good He does on our behalf because of His mercy, love, and forgiveness.

It is believed that Martin Luther said,

"Beautiful music is the art of the prophets that can calm the agitations of the soul; it is one of the most magnificent and delightful presents God has given us."[15] Steve's soul definitely needed calming.

The next morning was an unforeseen experience for which I was unprepared. In his brokenness, Steve came home and wept in my arms on behalf of his loss. Compassion welled up in my heart, and I felt his pain. I also wept. Indescribable love and forgiveness poured into my heart towards Steve. A couple of days later he came for dinner to see the boys . . . and never left. "She" left this earth, and Steve came home. Some things you can't explain or understand. God can turn a situation around in a moment.

There was only one chance to share the salvation message with one who would soon face eternity. God arranged the meeting. His unfailing love reaches out to the lost. No words can describe how thankful I am to have obeyed. It takes only a breath to call upon His name. I hope to see her in heaven. Eternity will tell.

Death and sorrow gave birth to reconciliation and joy. A beautiful season in our marriage. As a result, we had an intimate wedding ceremony with the renewal of our vows in which my parents and older sister, Claudia, flew to Hawaii to celebrate with us! The dying flames of a turbulent marriage rekindled which sparked a desire for us to share this overflow of love through adoption. Thus, Mindy became our third child, our daughter, "reborn" into our family when she was three-and-a-half years young. Our family was complete.

---

15  Martin Luther King, Jr., "Beautiful music is the art of the prophets that can calm the agitations of the soul; it is one of the most magnificent and delightful presents God has given us," *AZ Quotes,* https://www.azquotes.com/quote/180787.

"Music is the soundtrack of our lives,"[16] according to Dick Clark. It is our joy to be God's instruments like in St. Francis of Assisi's prayer.

*Lord, make me an instrument of thy peace;*
*Where there is hatred, let me sow love;*
*Where there is injury, pardon;*
*Where there is doubt, faith;*
*Where there is despair, hope;*
*Where there is darkness, light;*
*Where there is sadness, joy;*
*And all for thy mercy's sake*
*O divine Master*
*Grant that I may not so much seek to be consoled as to console;*
*To be understood as to understand;*
*To be loved as to love;*
*For it is in giving that we receive;*
*It is in pardoning that we are pardoned;*
*And it is in dying that we are born to eternal life.*

The new sound will be different from the old. Open your ears and heart to hear the new sound. *Love Beyond* the music.

---

16  Dick Clark, "Music is the soundtrack of our lives," *GoodReads*, https://www.goodreads.com/quotes/284082-music-is-the-soundtrack-of-our-lives.

# CHAPTER 5

# COURAGE AND SERENITY

## *Love Beyond Your Limitations and Fear*

*"Life is a balance of holding on and letting go."*[17]
—RUMI

O h, to escape from the complexities and heartbreaking challenges of life! Sometimes I wish I were a turtle. On my usual walks at Freestone Park or the Riparian Preserve, I often see turtles hanging out on a big rock alongside the edge of the lake. Each looks so slug-gardly and relaxed (although I'm not advocating laziness). With its neck stretched out to catch the sun's rays, it stays in that fixed position for quite a while as I've stood by, observing its idleness. Then, at will, the

---

17 Rumi, "Life is a balance of holding on and letting go," *QuoteFancy*, https://quotefancy.com/
quote/905265/Rumi-Life-is-balance-of-holding-on-and-letting-go.

turtle goes into hiding as it tucks its arms, legs, and head inside its shell cave and becomes oblivious to the craziness of the world.

> Sometimes I'm not up,
> but down.
> Sometimes I'm not high,
> but low.
> At times, I don't feel like smiling,
> When it's easier to wear
> a frown.
> Sometimes it's hard to keep going
> When I feel like quitting,
> But then I hear a song:
> "Hold on
> Just a little bit longer
> You're getting stronger."
> Breathe a deep sigh
> of relief.
> Life is so very brief
> 'Til these woes all pass away.
> So, press on to make it through
> another day.

## TAKE COURAGE

Just to get out of bed some mornings takes courage because you know what the day holds. Courage is defined as "the quality of mind or spirit that enables a person to face difficulty, danger, or pain without showing fear." However, I've done more things afraid rather than unafraid.

Courage isn't necessarily acting in the absence of fear; instead, courage confronts the faceless fretful monster with bulldog tenacity! You must aggressively bulldoze straight over fear. If you wait until fear is eliminated before making a decision or taking action, you may be waiting indefinitely, doing nothing to achieve success or to move forward. Stuck. Stagnant. At what price are you willing to let fear stay in the driver's seat? Its intention is to frighten you into submission, causing you to lose confidence in your ability to do what's necessary.

*Courage isn't necessarily acting in the absence of fear; instead, courage confronts the faceless fretful monster with bulldog tenacity!*

Confronting fear takes boldness, and you can overcome it through the power of the blood of Jesus instead of being enslaved by it. Growth doesn't happen in the comfort zone. The unknown and unfamiliar aren't comfortable. Seek counsel from God and trustworthy friends, keeping in mind God's plan is always to rebuild, repair, and restore, whenever possible.

## LET GO OR HOLD ON?

Elisabeth Eliot once penned:

> *The growth of all green living things wonderfully represents the process of receiving and relinquishing, gaining, and losing, living and dying. . . . There is no ongoing spiritual life without this process of letting go. At the precise point where we refuse, growth stops. If we hold tightly to anything given to us, unwilling to let it go when the time comes...or unwilling to allow it to be used as the Giver means it to be used, we stunt the growth of the soul. It is easy to make a mistake here. 'If God gave it to me,' we say, 'it's mine. I can do what I want with it.' No. The truth is that it is ours to thank Him for and ours to offer back to Him, ours to relinquish, ours to lose, ours to let*

*go of—if we want to find our true selves, if we want real life,*
*if our hearts are set on glory.*[18]

How do you choose? To let go requires trusting; to hold on requires trusting. Either decision requires courage, especially when the final outcome is unknown. Don't get bogged down with analysis paralysis. As God works in accordance with His perfect plan, His ways, strategies, and designs are unique in each life with each individual specifically on His mind (see Jeremiah 29:11).

Due to our marital problems, some friends said, matter-of-factly, I ought to let go of the marriage. But that option and their reasoning went contrary to my convictions as I knew God's will in my situation. There were times I said, "God, I just want out—I want a godly marriage." Oftentimes, it would have been easier for me to let go and walk away from the marriage since there were biblical reasons to do so, but God's ways and plans are perfect, even when they don't make perfect sense to us.

I didn't feel at all courageous, as with every step of obedience, a trail of tears was left behind. Yet, I held onto Romans 8:37 (KJV): "In all these things we are more than conquerors through him [Christ] that loved us." "In all these things" includes everything thrown at you. There are no hard-and-fast rules to know which choice is better: letting go or holding on. But there are tried-and-true disciplines to help you along the way: meditating on the written Word, hearing the voice of God, remembering past victories, praying, heeding godly counsel, and communing with Christian friends who come alongside you with encouragement and words of wisdom. Then, resolute and unswerving, you can move forward with confidence. Celebrate each timid step as an overwhelming victory, regardless of how insignificant it may look or how astronomical the problems appear.

Consider the following verses from the second half of Psalm 119:30-32 (MSG, emphasis added):

---

18 Elisabeth Elliot, *Passion and Purity: Learning to Bring Your Love Life under Christ's Control* (Ada, Michigan: Revell, 2013), Chapter 38.

*Barricade the road that goes Nowhere. Grace me with Your clear revelation. I choose the true road to Somewhere. I post Your road signs at every curve and corner. I grasp and cling to whatever you tell me; GOD, don't let me down! I'll run the course You lay out for me, if You'll just show me how.*

### *God delights in pointing the way! All we have to do is to follow the signs.*

God delights in pointing the way! All we have to do is follow the signs. However, despite the many road signs, the mind sometimes wanders along dusty roads and then parks in a godforsaken lot. At that desolate place, a compulsion further drives us to forage through the ruins of yesterday, which is nothing but a rubbish heap of disappointments, regret, and seeming defeat. Guilt leads you to question whether something of value was overlooked or perhaps you misjudged or reacted prematurely. You start taking on blame and saying "I could've" or "I should've."

Therefore, you painstakingly go through yesterday's woe-be-gone stuff. Instead of letting it go, you want to reclaim what was discarded, so you make excuses and justify its necessity. Precious time is wasted as you meticulously clean and shine your trophy, which is a tangible daily reminder of yesterday, so it can be displayed again in a prominent place. The clutter of yesterday's mess continues to grow instead of shrinking. I've been there, physically and/or emotionally, plopped in the middle of a pile of yesterday's quagmire of confusion, groaning, "Woe is me!"

*"Reflect upon your present blessings, of which every man has many; not on your past misfortunes, of which all men have some."*[19]
—CHARLES DICKENS

---

19 Charles Dickens, "Reflect upon your present blessings, of which every man has many; not on your past misfortunes, of which all men have some," *BrainyQuote*, https://www.brainyquote.com/quotes/charles_dickens_121978.

When you find yourself *there* again, wanting to pick up the past, remember that in doing so you are very likely to miss the new thing God is doing right in front of you. God commands us to "forget the former things; do not dwell on the past" (Isaiah 43:18). God will make a better life than the one you left.

Are you a fixer? Sometimes you want to fix the problem, so you don't let go until, finally, you get exasperated enough and realize God can do a better job than you! Or out of sheer desperation, you let go because of dire consequences you might otherwise have to face. "Let go and let God" will allow you to gain "the more" He has for you. Releasing the burden of trying to be the answer brings freedom. Ask God for guidance and strength to do what you cannot. He longs for you to look to Him for help in your time of need.

In a world that prides itself on self-reliance and independence, being led by Holy Spirit is countercultural. It is an acknowledgment that true strength doesn't come from one's own ability to navigate through life alone but, rather, with God's wisdom and godly counsel (see James 1:5 and Proverbs 15:22).

## POLLUTANTS

You are not to be a reservoir but a flowing river and crystal-clear stream. The stream remains pristine as you daily choose to not allow the pain of the past to poison your present or your future. Therefore, guard your heart and mind against pollutants such as unforgiveness, resentment, and bitterness that would contaminate all your relationships. Forgiveness is a choice, not an option.

Leave behind the heavy and darkened thoughts that keep you from seeing the breathtaking beauty of the most important time—this morning.

To aid in the tough decision-making process of holding on or letting go, consider the following: Don't allow fear to rule your decision. Fear, itself, is the biggest culprit in life's troubles. It hinders the way of wisdom, compassion, and gratitude and can make you cling to an unhealthy past because you're afraid of the unknown future. Your emotions shouldn't validate a decision. Keep a forgiving heart to avoid a vengeful attitude in trying to get even. "If only" or "I wish" will keep you dissatisfied. Avoid the blame game, perfectionism, overthinking, negativism, making a snappy or impulsive decision, choosing something because you're expected to, comparisons, and excuses that take you away from what you need to face. Don't settle for less by default. It is a waste of time to fight for things that no longer matter.

My friend, Sonny Martinez, shared these encouraging words:

*Letting go is not giving up. By letting go we are free. We only fail by holding on. Move forward, keep an open mind, and look back only to see where you have been, not to see what you might have left behind. Remember yesterday, cherish today; by letting go, we move toward tomorrow. Hope you are doing well. Keep the faith.*

*Serenity isn't the freedom from the storm but the peace within the storm.*

Serenity isn't the freedom from the storm but the peace within the storm.

When I'm at the end of my rope, I hold on to the God of all Hope. Serenity, calm, and tranquility come in knowing God got me through that; therefore, He can get me through this. It manifests as you take courage to pay more attention to God's voice than the opinion of others. Abandoning your past is to leave your future in God's hands and devote the present fully and completely to the Lord, bringing contentment and serenity. You can always refer back to Jeremiah 29:11 to be reassured God has good plans for you.

You may feel your problem is too great and your heart unfixable. The Breton Fisherman's prayer expresses the same feelings: "Dear God, be good to me; the sea is so wide, and my boat is so small." The good news is you have a boat and a paddle. However, in this infinite ocean of undulating waves, raging torrents, and powerful undercurrents, it's ludicrous to think any one of us fully knows how to completely chart the course we're following. You give your best and paddle as hard as you can but only have control of your own paddle. Without any control over the buffeting waves of the sea, there's no guarantee you won't get knocked into the surf, though you can learn to swim in case that happens. What's the moral of this story? Learn to swim before getting in the boat, or at least grab a life vest. Know when to hold on to your paddle and when to let go and jump into the water!

One of my life experiences—not so funny at the time—now makes me chuckle. When living in Guam, I took an adventure trip with Steve to New Zealand. One of the activities was to go river rafting in the rapids. The raft was large enough to accommodate several people—I don't remember exactly how many . . . but about eight. Horrendous, humongous, and continuous waves poured more water into the boat than out. I found it impossible to stay on the seat as I kept slipping, scooting, sliding, and slithering onto the floor of the boat. After several failed attempts at trying to get back up and staying firmly seated, I finally realized the boat's sole was the safest place for me (and all other passengers) to be, so I let go of my pride and settled down on the floor where I remained for the rest of that adventurous excursion. From my low vantage point, it was impossible to see or prepare for the oncoming crashing waves. Sometimes you have to find a place of survival and just hold on until the ride is over.

In John Maxwell's book, *Success 101*, he says there are four kinds of people when it comes to relationships. You decide whether to hold onto or let go of particular relationships.

1) Those who add something to life (we enjoy them).

2) Those who subtract something from life (we tolerate them).

3) Those who multiply back into our lives (we value them).

4) Those who divide something in life (we avoid them)[20]

Grasp the following truths I found in Roy Lessin's devotional *As You* (author emphasis added). Hold onto them. Let them guide you. Put them into practice.

> *As you **lean** upon the Lord, lean trustingly.*
>
> *As you **call** upon the Lord, call confidently.*
>
> *As you **wait** upon the Lord, wait quietly.*
>
> *As you **depend** upon the Lord, depend completely.*
>
> *As you **cast your cares** upon the Lord, don't take them back.*
>
> *As you **look** upon the Lord, you will see the face of a caring Father.*
>
> *As you **make a decision**, have His approval.*
>
> *As you **hear God's voice**, listen with your heart.*
>
> *As you **abide** in the vine, you won't produce sour grapes.*
>
> *As the **deer pants** for water, let righteousness create your thirst.*
>
> *As you **ask God** for help, know how helpless you really are.*
>
> *As you **ask God** to weed the garden of your heart, allow Him to pull up the roots.*
>
> *As you **use your hands** to serve the Lord, moisten them with the lotion of joy.*
>
> *As you **pray**, speak as a child, not as an orator.*[21]

Declare with confidence: "Today I am happy and ready to let go of what's gone. I am content and grateful for what remains. With great anticipation and expectation, I look for what is on its way!" *Love Beyond* your limitations and fear!

---

20  John C. Maxwell, *Success 101: What Every Leader Should Know* (New York, NY: HarperCollins Leadership, 2008).

21  Roy Lessin, "As You," *Thoughts about God*, 20 Sept. 2022, https://thoughts-about-god.com/blog/roy-lessin_as-you/.

# CHAPTER 6

# FINDING ME

## *Love Beyond a False Identity*

*"A good name is more desirable than great riches."*
—PROVERBS 22:1 (NIV)

## WHO AM I?

In one particular round of marriage counseling sessions, it was suggested I change the way I dressed to more of Steve's liking to accommodate him. Become more casual. Wear T-shirts (with holes in them—before that was fashionable). Definitely, forget the makeup. That image was not me. It was an imitation of someone with whom Steve was involved. I complied and discovered what it was like being uncomfortable in my own skin. Copying someone else makes you question everything about yourself. That experiment was short-lived. I was falsifying who I was and didn't know who I was becoming. If I'm not who I think I am, who am I? It was a ridiculous solution for a happier marriage when, instead, Steve's opprobrious behavior needed to stop.

*Time is of the essence for growth and development of any relationship, but time alone doesn't necessitate growth.*

I found myself trying so hard to be something more, or different, obsessed with trying to please him, which evolved into a performance-based relationship just to be accepted and loved. I clung to the hope that eventually Steve would learn from his mistakes—not that he would grow out of them but grow through them—and assume responsibility for his unfaithfulness; but time alone doesn't necessitate growth. A desire and effort are both required to effect change in an individual. Nothing in the world would ever have been enough to satisfy his addiction to pornography. Transformation from the inside out—a change of heart—is essential, but only God can do that when a person is willing to surrender his weakness. My reaction to a lack of love and acceptance was passivity with a gnawing sense of insecurity. While I never lost sight of my values, faith, and identity in Christ, on the human level it was difficult as a wife who was rejected and unvalued. I was left with a gaping hole in my heart while gasping for love.

### "Dago" and "Chris"

Growing up, I was a happy little daddy's girl, who knew she was loved a lot! He dubbed me "Dago." It was my first endearing nickname and is ironic since Merriam-Webster defines it as an "insulting and contemptuous term for a person of Italian descent." Figure that one out! My pet name made me feel really special and proud of my Italian daddy. Everybody else just called me "Chris," a shortened version of Christina.

### "Christina"

As a teenager, I understood the significance of the name, Christina, which further bolstered my confidence in knowing I was made in

God's image with a God-given destiny and purpose for my life. What does the name Christina mean? It means "a Christian" or "follower of Christ" in ancient Greek and "anointed one" in ancient Hebrew. For me, it speaks of royalty as being a daughter and follower of King Jesus. At a very young age, my identity was anchored in Christ (see Hebrews 6:19).

*Pet names do not determine the outcome of your life or dictate your destiny.*

Perhaps you had a pet name. My name made me feel special and valuable, but names in themselves are not the measure of who you are. Pet names do not determine the outcome of your life or dictate your destiny. If you were raised in a loving family and healthy environment at home, be extremely grateful for the smiling memories it brings, for many ladies have suffered much due to a lack of love in dysfunctional homes. Knowing this truth gave impetus for writing my story to encourage you because regardless of your past, God has an amazing and abundantly wonderful life for you! I want you to believe it to be so. God is a loving heavenly Father.

For some, this subject only unveils hurtful memories associated with rude and derogatory names, slurs, or negative comments that followed you throughout life. Wherever there was a lack of love or truth, the empty space was filled with painful memories hidden behind deep, dark deceptions of worthlessness. You were not enough, and you'd never measure up. Because of real or perceived rejection, you felt insecure, believing you were insignificant. As a result, you became your worst critic with doubt and uncertainty as to who you really were. In an attempt to shield yourself from deeper wounds, impenetrable walls were erected to protect yourself from hurt and shame while compulsion and desperate hope drove you to strive for perfectionism to please others.

These attempts may bring temporary relief but will never bring healing to a wounded heart.

Yet, the wonderful news is that you are not a mistake and the truth of who you are is revealed in God's Word, not in the opinion of others. His hand formed you. He watched you in utter seclusion in the dark of your mother's womb as you were being formed. By His choosing and design, you are wonderfully complex and beautiful. God's marvelous "workmanship" is to be compared with no one else. You are unique. Don't try to be like the rest of "them." You need not try to win God's heart because He loves you perfectly and completely and knows you by name. His thoughts toward you are so very precious and can't be numbered or counted because they are more numerous than the grains of sand! (see Psalm 139:1-18)

## MUST I ALWAYS BE SOMEBODY ELSE'S SOMEBODY?

At a young age, thankfully, my identity as a Christian was established spiritually due to a godly foundation. Yet, for almost forty-three years, I was clearly marked as "Steve's wife." Our life revolved around his career and friends. My personal life and activities involved church and ministry in which he did not participate. It created a void in my life, an imbalanced relationship. I think of the frog in a pot of water on the stove—the temperature gets hotter until, finally, the boiling water kills the frog. That sounds rather morbid, but my point is I didn't realize I was losing myself throughout our marriage because I believed I fell short of what Steve wanted or needed as his wife. Thus, for years, I was known as "Steve's wife," my *role* in life, and I accepted it willingly.

## TELL THE TRUTH

On the TV show "To Tell the Truth," four celebrity panelists question three contestants (read aloud by the show's host) to determine which contestant a story is about. Each challenger, when asked his name, would state the central character's true name. The two impostors would lie their way through the game while the "real" character told the truth. The panelists voted, and at the end, the host asked, "Will the real (person's name) please stand up?" Maybe you've played the game unconsciously, and you've tried to imitate someone else. God gently peels back the layers until the real you is revealed, because it's you He loves. *Don't try to fit in—you were born to stand out!*

*Don't try to fit in—you were born to stand out!*

## FROM A CARNIVAL MAZE TO AMAZEMENT!

Did you ever go into a carnival fun house with a maze of mirrors? This was a very popular attraction at carnivals and fairs. The idea was to walk through corridors, a maze of mirrors laid out like a puzzle, as you tried to find your way to the exit. Instead of a regular mirror that reflects a perfect image, the carnival mirrors distorted figures in humorous ways or depicted extremely grotesque and creepy reflections of yourself.

Unfortunately, when your personhood has been cruelly and verbally attacked, those kinds of false images can so distort the true picture in your own mind, that when you look in a regular mirror, all you see are imperfections and believe the ugly lie. We all do it, right? Every wrinkle gets magnified a hundred times greater as we scrutinize ourselves; the mirror can be our worst enemy! Except for the dire consequences of seven years of bad luck, I might have bashed it with a hammer! (Just kidding—but I did bash myself!)

The wrong image and perception you see aren't the end because the impact of God's amazing love and unconditional acceptance has the ultimate power to bring a breakthrough to your broken image. Every human being is made in God's image (see Genesis 1:27); therefore, you possess an innate value beyond anything else. Life is sacred from the moment of conception to the moment of death. How profound and beautiful is your uniqueness—the one and only you! To truly realize and grasp the truth of who God made you to be and to fully step into His purpose is life's greatest privilege.

## NONDESCRIPT OR NAMELESS

Here's a fun idea that could help change your feeling of being nondescript or nameless and give you a nickname. It's my personal little game or experiment for which an explanation and description follow. Others see us differently than we see ourselves as they peer through a different lens, so I've had fun asking friends to give me a nickname. The rule was that they couldn't call me by anyone else's name, or a generic, overused nickname attached to just anyone, such as "Baby" or "Honey," which I considered mindless and meaningless. It wasn't an option.

As I reviewed the list of names that friends had given me, a plethora of memories swirled in my head, spilling over into a mixed brew of emotions and a time of reflection. To revisit friendships in this way has been an interesting experience. I pondered each name's uniqueness, the season of my life I was in during that time, the purpose for which it was intended, what I learned from it, and its influence on my life (both positive and negative). Just like life, it's been a roller coaster ride with ups and downs, sharp curves, excitement, and frightfully wild and crazy times! Yet, all have been meaningful and significant in my life story. It's like wearing a different hat. You're the same person but accessorized in a different way.

What I've learned about myself is that I am an outrageous and fierce champion of love!

Just look at the list of names my friends gave me:

Christina, A.K.A.—Ducky, Christy, Pulsar (a favorite), Crisco (a slick Italian!), Nova, Firecracker, Fireball, Fire Starter, Sunbeam, Stardust, Hippie Chick, Chick-a-Dee, Wildflower, Energizer Bunny, Moonbeam,

Sunshine, Vibrant Beauty, Songbird, Queenie, Baby Cakes, Hot & Spicy, Chickie, PG13, Timex, Kitten, Buttercup, Desert Star, Mini, Sweets, WWW (Wild Wonder Woman), Chrissy, Sweetness, and Angel. But my given name—Christina—aptly and genuinely describes the heart and soul of who I am—a "follower of Christ." It is my true identity, for which I am so very thankful!

It's amazing how one term of endearment can touch a heart. Out of curiosity I looked up many of these idioms. Fire Starter was an especially interesting one because I had my personal opinion about its (biblical) meaning and, sure enough, it was confirmed by Google: Fire-starters are those who ignite, breathe upon and fan the flames of revival, restoration, transformation, and advancement of the kingdom of God. A further search, "Clarity on Fire" mentioned "the name implies that one is driven by an internal fire, a deep craving to create, transform, and shake things up."[22] Besides the acceptable affirmations above, maybe ask yourself "why" that name was given if there are some you question. Is there something you can improve upon? On a day when you don't feel great about yourself, choose a pet name, and perk up. Just be sure it's positive, uplifting, and doesn't conflict with how God would see you. Have fun with it!

## ABCs

Robert Schuller wrote a book titled *Believe in the God Who Believes in You.*[23] It sparked another creative way to affirm yourself because it revolves around what you believe about yourself. In this game, you declare ABC affirmations about yourself. Go crazy with it! It really helps to push back the negative stuff and bring the positive to the front. You can even learn some new words and descriptions about yourself. Say it! Write it! Believe it! Live it! Below is just a portion of my list, although I

22  "The Passion Profile Quiz," *Clarity on Fire*, https://clarityonfire.com/quiz/.
23  Robert H. Schuller, *Believe in the God Who Believes in You* (India: Orient Paperbacks, 2006).

have affirmations that span from A-Z! You'll be intrigued and encouraged through the discovery of finding yourself.

**A:** Ablaze, Amenable, Agreeable, Assiduous

**B:** Blessed, Bright, Beneficent, Buoyant, Benevolent

**C:** Charismatic, Christian, Considerate, Compassionate, Cooperative, Cheerful

**D:** Dedicated, Delightful, Dependable, Dauntless, Devoted

**E:** Energetic, Enthusiastic, Ebullient, Encourager

**F:** Fierce, Fiery, Faithful, Fun, Forgiven

## INNER BEAUTY

Theodore Roosevelt has often been credited with saying the following: "Comparison is the thief of joy." Whether he said it or not, it is totally true. So, it is better that we be genuine—real, actual, sincere, honest, and authentic—as 1 Peter 3:3-4 (NIV) describes:

> *Your beauty should not come from outward adornment, such as elaborate hairstyles and the wearing of gold jewelry or fine clothes. Rather, it should be that of your inner self, the unfading beauty of a gentle and quiet spirit, which is of great worth in God's sight.*

(There was no mention of shoes! LOL!)

Do some soul-searching by asking yourself these questions.

How do you feel you measure up?

Who or what influences the way you perceive yourself?

What are the expectations you have set for yourself?

Whom or what do you allow to label you?

The qualities of the inner life—having a heart of compassion, kindness, humility, gentleness, and patience (see Colossians 3:12)—are the very core of yourself, but without knowing your intrinsic value, you can be easily persuaded to conform to the opinion of others, which can be blatantly false.

# To have a beautiful life, decide to make everything around you beautiful.

What image do you portray? Women do well at fixing themselves up, primping, and looking great, but if the external is the prominent image displayed, is that the real person? An attempt to cover up or compensate for inward insecurities by adorning the outside may temporarily help in feeling good about yourself, but it's not a solution. Clothing and trendy outfits eventually get outdated. Wrinkles happen! Step aside and take a look inside to realize the truth of to whom you belong and who created you. Instead of keeping up with the constant trends in fashion and makeup, allow the Creator to change you into the beautiful and unique person He created you to be.

It blows my mind that God knows the very numbers of hair on our heads! That's how much He cares and knows about you. Can He not be trusted in His perfect design when He made you? If you're like me, when you've been out, dressed nicely, and you finally get home, you can hardly wait to disrobe and change into your "stay-at-home-comfy-not-so -cute-clothes." Just be raw and real. Just be you. Allow yourself to be found. Someone's looking for you.

It's like that song by Mark Schultz. Its title is "You Are a Child of Mine," and it describes a conversation between a person and God. The person starts with how he is struggling with the messages that the world bombards him with. However, he chooses to believe what God says. Before and after all, he is God's child, His design, and free in Him.

When you identify with Christ, it makes an identity statement about who you are. Let the imprint of God's hand upon your heart mark your identity. He says to you in Isaiah 43:1 (NLT): "I have called you by name." Forsake a false identity! *Love Beyond* what others call you and to what God calls you! His Masterpiece!

# CHAPTER 7

# THAT PLACE

## *Love Beyond Loneliness*

*Can't ignore the feeling*
*Or deny the disappointment—*
*My heart is hurting and my head reeling*
*Because, here, I find myself again*
*Going through too much pain.*
*But this is not where I'll stay.*
*Take me back to that place*
*Where I'm held in the grip of Grace.*

**A**mnesia might sometimes be welcomed. Just flip a switch to turn it on and off at will when you want to forget a memory—not necessarily just bad memories but sentimental ones that break your heart. One of the most painful experiences in life is loneliness. It can't be minimized because it can take you out. It's not marginalized as it can happen to anyone, anytime, anywhere. And my soul was wrecked.

With the passing of time, a trend of infidelity, lack of commitment, pornography, excessive drinking, and personal attacks on my Christian beliefs became more frequent. Humor became sarcasm. Contention grew stronger as Steve's heart became more hardened against Christ. With these vices in his life, I could never have been enough. There was more than sufficient time and ample forgiveness for him to become the husband he promised to be, but light invades and exposes dark spaces (see Ephesians 5:11-13). On several occasions, Steve explicitly said, "I love you. I just can't stand who you are." He was targeting my Christianity.

## FROM BLISS TO THE ABYSS

*A day came forty-two-and-a-half years later*
*When my beloved said, "I'm no longer happy.*
*There's another with whom I'd rather be,*
*And I finally have the courage to leave."*
*On that grievous day when he did part*
*I was left behind with an aching heart.*
*In the deepest anguish of soul, I cried,*
*"O, God, how can this be?*
*Forever he promised to love only me!"*

Divorce is a process of erosion . . . slow and painful. Marriage, which was once my greatest joy and peak of life, became quicksand—a mockery—that gradually sank me to the lowest depth of despair. Despite the pitfalls, I had not anticipated the end of our marriage when life got turned upside down. Memories were strewn all over my cluttered mind as the wreckage of what I thought was once an impenetrable castle came crashing down.

When Steve moved out, this invisible, faceless haunting creature called loneliness crept in and seemingly lurked around every corner, clawing at my heart, ripping it apart. At home, in the deadening silence, its ominous presence was felt and especially magnified.

## SURROUNDED BY LOVE
## AND SELDOM ALONE

For my entire life, I had never lived alone. Home was a happy and safe place with much affection and laughter, with five siblings. I had a roommate at Oral Roberts University, and then I married and along came three children. Even when Steve strayed and we weren't so "together," we were in the same house (most of the time). His body was present even if his thoughts were scattered elsewhere. The impact of the divorce was catastrophic in my life. Alone! The quiet exacerbated the feeling of loneliness.

A song I played over and again was "The Hurt and the Healer," a song by Mercy Me. It encapsulated my feelings so well. The lyrics describe how someone must submit to their suffering to experience God's glory. They are hurting intensely, feeling alone, as if part of them has died, but in the arms of the Healer, life is breathed back into their hearts, their fears and tears are taken, and they experience God's majesty and grace. It is only when their hurt and the Healer collide that anything makes sense. Only when the Healer says, "It's over now," is it over.

Loneliness isn't equated with being alone since it can emerge even in the midst of a large crowd. It's a sense of feeling disconnected. Unnoticed. Unimportant. Perhaps ignored. I remember looking around at happy people and thinking, *If you only knew how sad I am and how disconnected I feel in the midst of all that's going on, you would take pity on me.* Elements of self-pity can do weird things to your emotions.

What do you do in that dreadful place of loneliness? Where do you go? Sometimes you have to get inside your head and examine thought patterns to see where they came from and where they're taking you. Ask yourself, *What or who was I thinking of that brought on this thought or feeling?* Discouraging and disparaging thoughts must be replaced. Things come into our lives by what comes out of our mouths (see Proverbs 23:7). You are what you think. The verse I lived by and slept with was Philippians 4:8 (AMP):

*Whatever is true, whatever is honorable and worthy of respect, whatever is right and confirmed by God's word . . . pure and wholesome . . . lovely and brings peace . . . admirable and of good repute; if there is any excellence, if there is anything worthy of praise, think continually on these things [center your mind on them, and implant them in your heart].*

Think about your thoughts! And turn them into prayers.

Thoughts are absolutely powerful and transforming. Adapting a positive biblical mindset and perspective inevitably leads to a much different, better, happier, and more peaceful path.

*Certain aspects of God's presence can only be experienced in a deserted, lonely place, when darkness and insecurity surround you.*

A song titled, "Mend My Broken Heart" by LifeBreakthrough expresses the pain that is felt in brokenness. Your heart may be broken into pieces, and you feel like a bird with broken wings unable to fly. Doubts now feel the empty space that once held dreams. Tears incessantly pour down like rain. Yet you keep believing for Jesus to mend your endless pain. Jeremiah 17:14 (author paraphrase) says, "God, pick up the pieces. Put me back together again. You are my praise!"

The feeling of loneliness can be so intense. It tends to magnify itself in despair or despondency in an attempt to be above what even God is able to do. When the soul is afflicted, there are ways to rise above or go through the situation when hope, based on God's Word, becomes your steadfast foundation of truth. God cannot lie. Although unseen, Christ is always with you and will never leave you nor forsake you. His very name, Emmanuel, means God is with you. Always. Because God is your refuge and strength (see Psalm 46:1), you can run to Him and find comfort. Just as you can sit in a chair and know it will support you, you can "rest your laurels" securely upon God's promises.

Allow your loneliness to create in you a deeper longing for God's presence. The need and desire for companionship drew me closer to His heart and friendship with Jesus became more intimate. He delights in us and sings and rejoices over us (see Zephaniah 3:17), so I started dancing with Him (at home). There were times when I looked directly in His eyes, and it seemed His face would shine upon me (see Numbers 6:25).

## COMBATTING LONELINESS

When you come face-to-face with a monstrosity, do you try to manage, maneuver, or manipulate the situation? Does it get the best of you?

Gratitude and self-pity cannot coexist. For a while, going out and seeing happy families together in a park, at a restaurant, at church, or wherever, created jealousy in my soul which made my heart sad and even angry because of the loss of generational ties and experiences of joy and life as they were meant to be, together, as a family. Initially, when I saw older couples holding hands, my first thoughts were self-centered: *I shouldn't be alone after all the years I devoted to "him." I should be walking hand-in-hand with my forever love!* Self-pity was spiraling me downward toward feelings of jealousy. Climbing out of a slippery pit of self-pity is difficult, but when you grab hold of obedience in an effort to emerge from the quagmire of loneliness, the hand of God will take hold of yours to pull you out of your slimy mess. Great joy does come through obedience even if your situation doesn't turn out the way you hoped it would.

Negative feelings and thoughts can be overcome by expressing happiness on someone else's behalf, and it was a principle I had to learn and practice consistently. I went on the offense and took faith walks looking for families in the park, sweethearts, and older couples, so I could demonstrate what I believed. To avoid the pitfall of jealousy, I began acting in faith by complimenting a mom or dad on bringing such happiness to their children which was evident in their laughter and bright smiles. In dying to my own desires, I could bless others. Without their knowledge, I also prayed for families as I passed them. This kept my heart from bitterness because blessing and bitterness don't mix! This simple outreach helped me combat loneliness. Moreover, if you have a healthy relationship with your family, enjoy them!

As your life is enriched through positive people, you, too, can seize the opportunity to sow seeds of kindness unexpectedly and be a positive influence on others with no strings attached. Still, another way to push back loneliness is by doing random acts of kindness. Extend a blessing to someone in the way you would like to be blessed.

Sometimes silence was overwhelming, so I made a lot of noise with a LOUD voice and outcry (as if He were hard of hearing!), "God, I'm lonely! Do You hear me?" There was a lot of emotion released in that outcry. Then, I would turn that complaint into praise and affirm God's Truth even if a gnawing feeling of loneliness remained on the inside. It took tenacity and a resolute decision to get past roadblocks and move forward to avoid sinking into a quicksand pit of isolation. Frequently, I praised my way out of loneliness and despair and into victory. Praise is the voice of triumph (see Psalm 47:1).

The best way to get out of self-pity is to think less of self and more of others. Do to others as you would have them do to you (see Luke 6:31). Any time you take your eyes off your problem and develop a thankful heart, there will be breakthrough as you push back the enemy. Gratitude will help you emerge from the quagmire of loneliness and live on the sunny side of life!

Emotional pain is real, but it must not run or ruin your life. Boldly proclaiming truth according to God's Word can radically change your outlook, even if circumstances remain the same. God thoughts replace the negative woe-is-me narrative. A willingness on your part is all God wants, and He'll give you all the help needed to overcome every adversity because you can do all things through Christ who strengthens you (see Philippians 4:13).

## THE ENCOUNTER

The heaviness and burden of carrying loneliness with many negative emotions such as fear, self-pity, and resentment was a heavy cloak that weighed me down tremendously and, although it was uncomfortable, I became somewhat accustomed to the feeling. Finally, one day I came to the end of myself. With no time to waste, I went straight to the point:

"God, we need to talk, and I have to hear from You. Either this faceless monster has to leave or I have to go. It's my home and I'm not leaving."

With an understanding smile, He reminded me, *I am Jehovah-Shammah. I Am There—always, and My angels remain on assignment.*

A bit impatiently I replied, "Okay . . ." I was really implying the question, "So, what's next?"

Admittedly, my attitude was not humble but rather demanding. I wanted to be rescued from this nagging loneliness.

"So, what must I do or not do to be rid of this haunting figure?"

Without a rebuke and with much patience, God responded lovingly, "*What you're doing right now is what you must do.*"

That made no sense. Quite perplexed, I asked, "And what is *this* that I'm doing?"

"*Coming to me. Asking for My help,*" He stated matter-of-factly. "*You have come to that place of desperation and readiness saying, 'I will not live like this anymore.' Ready to hear My voice, not only with your ears but your heart as well. My child, have you noticed the quietness here—away from the many distractions?*"

My thought was, *But I'm trying to get away from the quiet and the aloneness.* I'd like a little more clatter . . .

As He knew my thoughts, a wide grin spread across His compassionate face as He tenderly spoke, "*My Little Bird, You need not fly away to find me. I am Jehovah-Shammah, already there, with you. You are never alone."*

As He drew me close, His breath was like a soothing breeze. I laid my head comfortably upon His shoulder as tears flowed in rivulets down my face and onto His robe. In the stillness, I could hear nothing but His heartbeat as I rested in His wraparound presence; then He lifted the hem of His robe, dried my salty tears, and calmed my fears. No longer was I afraid of loneliness because being alone with Him was dearer than anything I could ever have imagined.

In that moment of contented peace, Father began singing over me and I was completely captivated. It was as if birds chimed in as all creation heard His voice reverberating throughout the atmosphere, spreading in all directions—to the highest mountain peak, beyond into the heavens, and below to the deepest valley. The prevailing mood was calm, peaceful, and reassuring. Heaviness had lifted and I felt as light as a feather.

## *Pure love drenched me; it was so refreshing.*

Now, pure love drenched me (according to 1 John 4, He IS love!); it was so refreshing. At the climax of the song, while still nestled in Father's arms, we conversed about the journey—the highs and lows, the difficulties, challenges, and victories celebrated, the sacrifice of love, the pathway to freedom through forgiveness, and His encouragement to, once again, dream big. Verses on wisdom encouraged me to remain focused on God's greatness and bigness, to stay on the straight and narrow path (see Matthew 7:14). His Word was a light unto my path, assuring me that I would get to the glorious end that is more wonderful than I have yet believed or imagined (see Psalm 119:10). At the end, He promised, Love is already waiting. My soul was revived, and my heart began to beat again. Maybe this little bird with a broken wing could fly after all!

This is a heavy topic. To lighten up a heavy heart, laughter can help. Loneliness is neither funny, nor is it a joke, but when feeling the doldrums, a healthy dose of laughter, even if it seems impractical and improbable at such a time, is like medicine to the soul. So, here's a joke to jumpstart your list: "I was lonely 'til I glued a coffee cup to the top of my car. Now everyone waves at me." I still laugh every time I recall this joke. Actually, I have left a cup of coffee on the roof of my car a couple of times, but it was definitely unintentional.

This verse can encourage you during those lonely times—Deuteronomy 31:8 (NIV) promises "The Lord Himself goes before you and will be with you; He will never leave you nor forsake you. Do not be afraid; do not be discouraged."

You are never alone when you are alone with God. For those who are feeling forgotten or lonely, I pray you'll find yourselves noticed and loved. Remember the eyes of the Lord are upon you. His love is expressed in unusual and unique ways. Embrace the quiet times, the stillness. Feel His presence and *Love Beyond* loneliness.

# CHAPTER 8

# GOD-AHA-MOMENTS

## *Love Beyond the Ordinary*

*"Never love anyone who treats you like you're ordinary."*[24]
—OSCAR WILDE

**Y**ou've likely experienced a "Eureka!" moment. The Greek term is *Heureka*, literally meaning "I have found it." I refer to these surprise moments of inspiration as God-AHA-Moments because He suddenly and unexpectedly showed up and showed off in the most unique ways to give insight and inspiration to restore and refresh my soul. His ways may seem uncharacteristic as to how you perceive God speaking. The following are examples that got me through the very challenging and extremely painful seasons of pre- and post-divorce. It was His way of loving me beyond the ordinary.

---

24 Oscar Wilde, "Never love anyone who treats you like you're ordinary," *goodreads*, https://www.goodreads.com/quotes/273844-never-love-anyone-who-treats-you-like-you-re-ordinary.

## BIRTHING THE NEW

A most unusual experience occurred at a moment when grief took me down and tried to take me out. For the last time, Steve had come to the house to get what was left of his belongings. Motionless, I stood transfixed in the garage, staring with glazed eyes of disbelief as he loaded his car to capacity to take his stuff and leave me behind.

Irritated, he said, "What are you staring at?"

Frazzled and bewildered, frankly, I wasn't sure why I was standing there watching him load his car with the last of his belongings. Was it to see him one last time before it was all to end? I felt numb and lightheaded, yet there was a dull ache. As he stuffed the last items in the trunk and got in his car to leave, I followed him and leaned against the open door to prevent him from shutting it; angrily, he told me to get out of the way.

"I will, but first, I have something to say," was my automatic robotic response. "Nobody will ever love you like I have."

It was impulsive. Once said, I moved out of the way as he slammed the door and took off. That was it. I took a few steps and pressed the garage door opener to close it and before I could get inside the house, I collapsed in a heap as life and breath seemed to have left my body. There was no consciousness of time as I curled up in a fetal position on the garage floor and began experiencing birth pangs. I've given birth. I know what it's like.

During this time of heaving and laborious breathing, I cried out in anguish, "Oh, God, what's happening?" I was unnerved.

*My child, you are experiencing the depth of grief that I, even now, as your Father, am feeling for your loss. You are dying to the past in order to give birth to the new.* His compassionate words pierced my heart deeply to begin healing the intense anguish. I experienced inexplicable groaning and moaning in the Spirit until all strength was gone, and I lay limp, oblivious to anything around me.

Then, I heard voices, soft and tender—whether I was in a conscious or sub-conscious state, I don't know—but I recognized my son Randy's voice. Next, I felt his strong arms gently scoop me up and hold me tightly and securely to his chest. His voice was calm, but I don't recall what he said. I only know he brought such comfort and reassurance at a time when I felt completely helpless. My two sisters, Claudia and Antoinette, who had also come to support me during this difficult day, followed Randy as he carried me and laid me carefully on my bed. They gathered around me, praying, as peace blanketed my entire being, and quietly, I rested in God's sweet presence.

## THE IMPORTANCE OF FOLLOW-THROUGH

A glance at my golf clubs stashed in a corner of the garage brought a barrage of remembrances of golf excursions in various elite places where I had enjoyed playing golf when married. The irony is my initial reason for learning to play golf was to avoid being a golf widow when Steve retired. Well, I'm not a widow.

As I stood there, sort of numb and somewhat angry while memories collided with reality, I wondered what life lessons were learned on the golf course. What I remembered most was the importance of "follow-through" on a swing—that I never quite mastered. Hmmm, then came a God-AHA moment—*Following through on a commitment makes you more reliable and dependable.* When it came to marriage, I followed through to the very end in loving my husband as Christ loved me, for better or worse. Quitting the marriage wasn't an option for me. It was never in my own strength or because of sheer determination that I stayed. Only through God's supernatural and abundant grace that He infused into my heart, was I able to love Steve unconditionally. I take no credit but accredit all goodness to the Lord Jesus Christ. Knowing that God knew my struggles and saw my faithfulness, brought joy to my heart.

## MOSAIC-STAINED GLASS DESIGN

On another occasion in the garage, God showed me a picture of an exquisite mosaic-stained glass design suspended in midair. Incredibly beautiful and brilliant. Then, without warning, it was suddenly blown to smithereens as splintered fragments fell in slow motion to the ground. What *was* a beautiful design had now become a heaping pile of unidentifiable jagged, broken pieces. Then, before my eyes, a transformation took place as all these tiny fragmented bits began lifting off the ground, floating lightly in mid-air, and reconnecting to recreate an even more elaborate and illustrious design than the original one. It even appeared more magnanimous and breathtaking. Father gave understanding to this scene.

The first mosaic-stained glass design was representative of my life when I was married which held wonderful possibilities and dreams. On the surface it appeared to be perfect. It looked stupendous, marvelous, and beautiful, but the Mosaic was *stained* with brokenness and infidelity. There was nothing to hold it together, and in the end, all that remained were a broken heart and broken dreams. Yet, what seemed obliterated and gone forever was recreated, far greater and more magnificent than the former. This thought has remained—*the old won't match the new—it will be very different.* I believe there's possibly more to be revealed about this. For now, I know my life is better, I am happier being me, and dreams are yet to unfold.

*The old won't match the new.*

## A DAGGER

As a speaker at Christian Women's conferences, I've had the opportunity to teach, encourage, and pray for many hurting women. But this time, I was not speaking, but an attendee, who was in great need of encouragement and strength for the battle raging in my life after the divorce. Soaking in God's presence while keenly listening to life-giving words during a dark season of my life gave me hope. At the conclusion of the service, a woman who was a complete stranger came up to me and said, "The Lord showed me a picture of your heart. Would you like me to tell you what I saw?" Of course, I did.

I don't remember verbatim what she said, but the following is taken from my journal notes, "I saw a dagger thrust into your heart that brought intense pain. Then a hand gripped the dagger and pulled it partially out. Again, the dagger was thrust into your heart. More grueling pain. It was pulled out, but still not all the way. This happened several times as the dagger was thrust into your heart and then pulled out but not completely. I could see your grimace of pain each time this occurred. There has been great agony and much pain inflicted over time. Then, one final blow came as the dagger was thrust deeper into your heart than all the other times. That's when I saw God's arm stretch toward you and His hand reached into your heart. He took hold of the dagger and pulled it completely out!" The lady then shared this message about the illustration: "God says to tell you, 'Never again will you ever suffer such pain.'"

He is aware of every infliction of pain and hurt thrust upon you. God sees every tear, knows everything, and fully understands and feels your heartache. His compassionate love flooded my soul with overwhelming gratitude! We triumph over the enemy of our soul and every adversity by the blood of the Lamb and by the word of our testimony. Right then was an opportunity to briefly share my story of how God's prevailing grace and supernatural forgiveness fortified me so I could remain in my marriage in spite of infidelity. God's preponderant love reaches beyond the shackles of our minds! He comes to your rescue. He loosens the bonds that have held you captive!

## A MISSING PUZZLE PIECE

While praying for my Knight in God's shining armor, I saw, suspended in mid-air, a humongous puzzle with hundreds of pieces. While I didn't notice what the actual puzzle picture was, I did notice one bare spot where a piece was missing. What surprised me was that one small blank space could be so conspicuous with hundreds of pieces assembled. It was an attention-getter, a God-AHA-moment that presented this thought: *the man I marry must be complete. If one piece is missing, he's not the one.* Not perfect. There are so many pieces that go into a relationship. For instance, he can be a jack-of-all-trades, have charisma, be Prince Charming, and have positive attributes. There can be an enjoyment factor in spending time together, and things might simply fit into place. However, the one most significant piece that can't be missing comes in the shape of a man's heart. One who is in hot pursuit of God. I might also add that attraction is important! Admittedly, I've tried to maneuver a piece of the puzzle in that blank space but no matter how I tried it just wouldn't work!

God, the great Puzzle Solver, keeps me in perfect "piece." My Kingdom man and I will be in complete harmony and one accord as we "run with perseverance the race marked out for us" (Hebrews 12:1, NIV).

## BOUQUET OF FLOWERS

I quoted Rumi earlier who said, "Life is a balance of holding on and letting go."[25] A beautiful bouquet of flowers vividly displayed this example of holding on far too long. One day, unexpectedly, a bouquet of flowers was delivered to my home—a pleasant surprise from someone I loved in a floundering relationship. As usual, I trimmed the stems, gingerly put them in a vase with water, added the little packet of nutrients, arranged them carefully, and then displayed them in a prominent place. Yet, within two days, the blooms faded, wilted, and dropped like dead flies. It was useless trying to salvage them.

---

25  Rumi, *QuoteFancy*.

The likeness between this dying bouquet and the longevity of the withering relationship in which we were pursuing marriage became quite evident, especially when this thought came to mind: *Stop trying to revive what's already dead.* The relationship had long ago shriveled up and was beyond repair. Watering a dead relationship is fruitless, futile, and foolish.

## MOON MAKER

There's nothing like being cradled by the moon beneath a velvety dark sky as fiery stars twinkle and pulsate above.

In Hawaii, where I lived for five years (married), there were many great adventures and experiences, yet I relish one distinctive, surreal memory—an extraordinarily beautiful sunset tour cruise in Honolulu aboard a very large catamaran that carried about twenty-five people. Sailing along Hanauma Bay, the ideal climate with mild temperatures, low humidity, and comfortable northeasterly trade winds was intoxicating. Its beauty was unparalleled. While approaching the shoreline, a majestic, exquisite scene appeared on the horizon as a brilliant full moon shone in all its glory upon Diamond Head crater. That romantic scene has remained vividly prominent in my mind's eye ever since.

However, on my lone journey, the lingering memory of its magnificence has saddened me on many beautiful moonlit evenings. One night, while driving, a splendid moon displayed itself directly above me, triggering my emotions so deeply I had to pull off to the side of the road where I cried out to God. "What am I to do with this memory that breaks my heart?"

The immediate response came as a gentle whisper: *"I am Moon Maker. I made the moon for you. Each time you see the moon lit up, remember that 'I love you to the moon and back.'"*

That thought has ever since kept me in love with the moon.

## LAUGHTER IS LIKE MEDICINE

A merry heart truly does good like medicine (see Proverbs 17:22). There are God-AHA-HA moments when the God of Surprises displays an uncanny sense of humor with witty wisdom—sometimes, in very unorthodox ways and methods because He delights in putting a smile on your face to lighten the load when life gets a bit unfunny. You can't put God in a box (or at least you shouldn't do so), and why would you want to? He's so big, grand, and creative with innumerable and inexhaustible thoughts and plans suited just for you. He knows precisely what touches your heart, gets your attention, makes you laugh, or causes you to seriously ponder a matter.

Enlightenment and inspiration help to navigate life differently and aid in making better decisions. When it comes to God's attributes and character, He is consistent and predictable—dependable, loving, faithful, and kind, so you don't have to wonder if He's going to be in a bad mood. When things get tough, get to laughing!

## THE UNREALISTIC AND POSSIBLY IMPOSSIBLE LIST

At one point I had a list of "must haves" and "must not haves" along with several preferences in choosing a man. Can you relate? Yes, of course you can. I'm neither for it nor against it—completely neutral, but this was my experience.

To preface this list, the first characteristic has always been a godly man who sincerely has a personal relationship with the Lord. To proceed, a friendly face with an irresistible smile (and nice teeth) was important, and a twinkle in the eye with a cheerful glance was even better. (Really, how does one gauge that?) Furthermore, my preference was an Italian man (I'm biased and they're romantic), with dark hair, deep brown piercing eyes, and tall (six feet!). One other important aspect was that he would be a musician—a guitarist would be great— who would sing and play love songs and worship songs—Jesus is important. This dream list was forged in my mind and heart as well as written down and memorized. However, a few years later God let me know how ludicrous it was. Remember His sense of humor?

To begin, Italians usually are not tall. (But I justified the fact that they're typically romantic.) Secondly, at my age, a man would have grey hair (or possibly not much hair at all), so dark hair wasn't likely unless it came in the way of a toupee or in a bottle. There were other "items," but this was enough to convince me of the unlikely possibility of meeting such a man, so my dream man went up in smoke, and I did away with the list and its other preposterous preferences. However, I know friends who had a very specific list, met the man to match it, and are happily married.

## NOT "EX" BUT "Y"

Two words caused me to cringe while struggling through the coming apart of my marriage: "divorce" and "ex." As with other statistics, they seemed to automatically be assigned to those of us who found ourselves in this category. Divorce made me feel ashamed. It was like I was wearing an emblazoned "D" across my chest that was grappling for my identity. I assigned "failure" to that word. I detested divorce, resisted it, and once upon a time, never believed I'd fall into that category. Yet, there seemed to be no avoidance of the word "divorce" as a signed, sealed, and done deal. (Irreconcilable differences are another "lie" that conceals the truth and reality behind the scenes of selfishness and lust.)

I resolutely refused the label "ex." It repelled, disgusted, and angered me. Can't you tell? Remember, these were tumultuous emotional disturbances in my life and sometimes I needed extra grace and mercy! So, wondering about options other than the "D" word, I presented my case before God. "Former husband" was definitely too formal. "Prince who became a frog" was maybe appropriate but not nice. "The man I shouldn't have married"? True, but too lengthy. So, I asked God, "What can I call Steve?" (God had nicer names than I did concerning Steve) and in my mind, I heard, *why*?

My reaction was immediate, "Because I don't like 'ex.'" That seemed obvious and reasonable enough.

Again, the question, *"Why?"*

"Well, WHY not?" I said in frustration.

This dialogue continued on in my mind without a resolution. A couple days later I shared this dilemma with my bank teller (a gal who had become a friend). Immediately, she had the answer, "Call him your 'Y' not your 'ex.'"

That was it! God had already given me the answer when He said "Y" but I misinterpreted it as a question. This story might seem trivial and completely irrelevant to you, but this issue was a thorn in my side and kept pricking my flesh. When it was finally resolved, there was relief tinged with a bit of humor as well.

## DUCKY

Ducky was my endearing nickname that Steve gave me after we were married. One day, while walking in a park, I couldn't help but notice the many ducks parading on the sidewalk squawking for a free handout from all the little kiddos. To avoid stepping on them I had to meander around them. There seemed to be just as many waddling in the pond. It brought to mind my past forgotten nickname, Ducky. I was clueless as to why he gave me that nickname and even asked him once. He didn't have an answer, and I couldn't recall any reason.

As I observed the ducks once again I wondered, although this time it was aloud as I often talked to God, "Why did 'he' call me Ducky?"

The unrestrained response popped into my head: "Because he was a quack."

That cracked me up! I couldn't make it up! It still makes me laugh and, thankfully, humor has gotten me through a lot of pain . . . even if others didn't think it was funny.

On another occasion, while walking at a different park (I gravitate to parks) on a lovely day, romance seemed to saturate the air. I wished for someone to be by my side as we held hands—chatting, smiling, laughing. It was a perfect day to revel in love, and I expressed my desire to God. Even so, my heart was grateful for His constant presence of which I have grown so much more aware in my singleness.

Before finishing my walk, I circled back to relax on a bench situated beneath a humongous pine tree with lengthy boughs sprawling across the pond and birds tweeting cheerful peeps while nestled in the swaying limbs. All the while I listened to a gentle waterfall cascading over rocks. What I fancied most, though, were darling ducks playfully skimming across the water, and to top off the entertainment, the sight of two ducks simultaneously submerged their heads in the water as their tail ends stood straight up, wagging furiously.

It was Father's quirky way of saying, "Remember, I'm head over heels about you!" Or head over tails?

I giggled and gave a nod to God, "Yeah, I know You are, and You sure have an unorthodox way of showing how much You care."

What a delightful experience. It's all about relationship. God is the love of my life. Are you allowing Him to be Your first love?

*It's all about relationship.*
*God is the love of my life.*

## ELDERLY COUPLE AT PANERA

A book has long been my favorite companion. Sipping on coffee while reading a book goes hand-in-hand, is a favorite pastime, and was particularly so while adjusting to the "single" status. Even if I didn't engage in conversation, frequenting coffee shops was a good way to simply be around people and maybe hear their conversations. Ha! I didn't really eavesdrop. One typical day while sitting on the outdoor patio at Panera

Bread reading a book—my usual routine—an elderly couple very slowly and carefully emerged from indoors. I couldn't help but observe them. In fact, I stared. They were smiling and holding onto each other so closely, and it tore at my heartstrings because that's what I always envisioned would be my and my husband's experience in marriage, holding onto each other while growing old together. As they passed my table, I commented on how sweet and happy they looked. For how long they'd been married, I don't recall, but they were in their eighties.

Then, in a spunky manner, his wife replied, "Oh, honey, we have to hold on tightly to hold each other up so we don't fall. If we do fall, we go down together." They both chuckled.

Trying hard to blink away some tears, I inadvertently said, "I recently went through a divorce."

Her tall, lanky husband was all of 6'3," and without a second of hesitation and with a twinkle in his eye, he bent all the way down, leaning within a few inches of my face until I felt his breath. Then, as an endearing father would speak, he said, "My dear, you are now FREE!"

It was so unexpected. I felt as though I'd come face-to-face with God who was assuring me, *It's okay. I'm here to walk this journey of freedom with you. I'll hold you up.* It was uncanny.

Keep your eyes open to see the invisible, your ears open to hear the unexpected, and your heart open to receive love.

As we are made in God's image and likeness, what we sense in emotions is, in essence, an image of what He feels. Scripture reveals God has emotions and feelings of compassion, joy, love, anger, and sorrow. God feels grief and laughs. These stories exemplify how He reveals Himself in so many different and unexpected ways, yet, quite naturally and simplistically. He cares ridiculously about every possible detail of your life—even in knowing the number of hairs on your head. Nothing is too insignificant, so give Him your cares, concerns, and worries. Life's frustrations give opportunity for God's grace. And laugh out loud with Him! To *Love Beyond* the ordinary is characterized by the unusual.

# CHAPTER 9

# SINGLENESS: THE BAD, THE UGLY, AND THEN THE GOOD

## *Love Beyond Your Status*

*"She" was many, not just one.*
*Although he still lived at home*
*And wore his wedding band,*
*For how long had she already*
*Occupied his mind?*
*He was within my reach, visible,*
*I could see him.*
*Yet, oblivious to my presence,*
*His thoughts gravitated toward her.*
*He was not the kind*
*Who wore his heart on his sleeve,*

*But I sensed his uneasiness—*
*When he was not being true or honest.*
*Sometimes he was giddy,*
*Like a kid in a candy store.*
*"Do I love my wife? Or love the other?*
*Do I stay, or do I go?"*
*He went back and forth from here to there,*
*Wandering and straying from home,*
*But eventually he'd find his way back—*
*Until one day, he passed through the revolving door*
*To take a walk and never returned.*
*But I knew he'd already left a long time ago.*

## THE BAD

If you're single, it's a *bad* idea to compare yourself with someone who's in a committed relationship. Being single has somehow become confused with being unsuccessful—especially if you're divorced—while being in a relationship equates to being successful. Where did that come from?

Relationships can be unsettling! Disturbing. Disappointing. Complicated. You get the idea. The transition from being married to becoming single wasn't simple like flipping a switch. No, sometimes, my switch flipped! To get real and transparent, I'm citing personal examples of my struggles, for inasmuch as I loved and trusted God through all the turmoil, I confess that sometimes I was feisty!

*Relationships can be unsettling! Disturbing. Disappointing. Complicated. You get the idea.*

For twelve years Steve and I lived in Guam. After his retirement from Continental Airlines in November of 2007, we returned to Louisville where I expected we'd live for the remainder of our lives. Yet, after the move, I maintained a close relationship with my Pastor Jon Pineda, and his wife, Sister Eva. At their request, we made a return trip to Guam on May 14th, 2012 so that I could be ordained as a missionary—as a teenager, I knew there was a calling on my life and I was excited about this opportunity. Humbly, I accepted the honor of serving God in whatever capacity He chose.

Although Steve didn't participate, he accompanied me on the trip. He did his thing, and I did mine, which was more often the norm.

The following are journal entries that demonstrate how life can brusquely change. From May to June 2012, in one month, everything in my world changed.

**Monday, May 14, 2012**

*Arrived in Guam after a long, but thankfully uneventful flight. Pastor Jon and Sister Eva have loaned us a car and given us accommodations at their house. Yesterday, I had the written test for ordination and have scheduled interviews tonight. It's amazing and fascinating what plans God has yet to unveil for me in this season of my life. After an early morning walk on Tumon Beach, a leisurely buffet breakfast at The Hyatt, and a relaxing afternoon, we have plans for dinner tonight with Mindy and her family after my interview. I'm living the abundant life in Christ!*

**Friday, June 17, 2012**

*The ordination in Guam held exciting possibilities with purpose and personal fulfillment, yet, as we returned to Guam, it remained a mystery as to how God's plan would unfold. Then, everything abruptly changed. One month later, in June 2012, Steve chose to walk out of our marriage. With one decisive action on his part, I went from being married for almost forty-three years to being single as divorce proceedings began soon after he left. How drastic things can become in such a short time. In the preceding month life held such a promising future full of wonder and great expectations. Now, there seemed to be no plan or certainty of tomorrow. It was like waking up to a different world—and it was different, completely unfamiliar to me, and unexpected. Steve and I traveled some rough and rocky roads in our marriage, but the road, eventually, always led home. This scenario was not part of the plan, at least not for me. Although my future was now uncertain, I held onto God's hand trusting Him to lead my every step—wherever that would be.*

Below are other posts on Facebook written after this upheaval:

**Saturday, June 23, 2012**

*"The umbilical cord has been cut! I'm free. I can breathe on my own and live again. I'm not alone! I'm not alone!"*

I was crying out to God in desperation and declaring what I knew to be true: God was always with me, but I *felt* so alone. Just taking the next breath was difficult. Yes, I was free, but I didn't want freedom. Where addictions ravaged and eventually destroyed our marriage, I wanted healing and restoration of my marriage with God at its center. I knew it was possible but it would require Steve to make changes—and that meant a change in his heart as well as breaking destructive patterns. Instead, he chose the way out and shut the door behind him.

**Sunday, June 24, 2012**

*I find myself at the foot of the Cross where tears of sorrow now mingle with tears of joy when once the well of joy seemed to have run dry. Weeping and laughter have converged on this twisting and spiraling course and become one. The heat of the desert is intense, but even the barren desert shall blossom, and it shall be, oh, so very beautiful!*

Interestingly, I spoke figuratively of being in the desert. And here I am, years later, in April 2023, living in the desert, and it's in full bloom as I write this! God holds tomorrow in His hands.

The pendulum swings. When great expectations turn upside down and life rapidly spirals downward, you may feel as though you'll never recover. A desert is a parched and barren place, yet, in the desolate place, "waters shall burst forth in the wilderness, and streams in the desert" (Isaiah 35:6, NKJV). God refreshes and restores your soul.

Below is a journal entry written during my time in Louisville—one year of being single but not yet divorced.

**Thursday, May 30, 2013**

*INTROSPECTION—DEMOLITION—RENOVA-TION—TRANSFORMATION*

*Holy Spirit—Inspector and Revealer of Truth. My heart can be a great deceiver, but all pretense is demolished as You bore a hole in the center of my heart and unearth its trappings. It's not about a remodeling job but total renovation and adjusting to change from a broken heart isn't convenient or comfortable, especially when "that" change is unwanted. It hurts and it's hard. What a mess things look like, including my life sometimes—but You have the blueprints and see the finished work. With an eye for perfection, You'll complete what you began. So, hammer away.*

What you consider to be the most important changes depends on what's going on in your life at any given time. How do you navigate through undesirable and, perhaps, irreversible circumstances for which you don't have a plan set in motion? What helped me was knowing God still had a plan for my future. The Word of God gave me hope and Jeremiah 29:11 was a verse I clung to. Regardless of your situation, God has a plan for you now and in the future to prosper you and give you a hope. Whatever He does is good and right even when what's happening in your life isn't good. Or right.

*Regardless of your situation, God has a plan for you now and in the future to prosper you and give you a hope. Whatever He does is good and right.*

The first time I filled out a form at an office, checking the box "divorced," was a bad experience. Something as little as checking a square really was disturbing! My new status was not a happy place—I was angry! We had been through hell and high water and survived, even thrived, after so many challenging situations. In parenting, we faced crises with our children (if you're a parent you know what I mean!), but we went through them together and came out on the other side together. The children grew and became independent. And I thought we would continue growing older together until death. Instead, our time together ended prematurely with the death of our marriage.

With all signatures in the designated places, at the stroke of a pen, my whole world changed. I was now Ms. If that weren't enough, our final "agreement" in the divorce decree also changed, but without my approval. What he promised was switched at the final moment of signing off. It was really bad—a raw deal—and dishonest. Nevertheless, in February 2014, during a cold, bleak winter in Louisville, the divorce decree was signed and finalized. It was a bad day, yet there was some relief that it was over.

Looking into a lone future was hard and disheartening. The TV show, The Lone Ranger,[26] was heroic but I didn't sense anything heroic in me. I felt like a failure! Plus, he had Tonto, his sidekick. I was alone. Initially, I didn't want to stick around here on earth. It was probably a bad request, but I made an appeal to God to take me to my eternal home which seemed like a far better place. I wanted to "fly away" as

---

26 *The Lone Ranger*, Hollingsworth Morse et al. (Sept. 15, 1949; Sterling, VA), Television.

the old song says. Accepting singleness was just plain hard, and some days, depression (and self-pity) assaulted me. But I recalled 1 Samuel 30:6 (ESV) that says, "And David was greatly distressed; for the people spoke of stoning him. . . . but David encouraged himself in the Lord his God." Well, thankfully, I wasn't about to get stoned in any way. I never lost faith, just good sense sometimes. Rather than God taking me home (escaping), He grew me deep in grace.

After the marriage door was closed, there was an open door to freedom, but there was no celebration at the time. At the closing of a door, you can stand and bang on it demanding that it open again! Yet, Jesus says He is the door (see John 10:9). He is the passageway and will see you through the transition. He never slams a door in your face—a closed door is never punishment. There's comfort in knowing He will escort you through the open door and continue to walk with you. You'll not walk alone.

## THE UGLY

There were tasks (they seemed more like tests) that now I had to take care of such as occasionally shoveling snow away from the front of the garage to get my car out. How dare he leave me out in the cold! With each shovel of snow, I had some very mean thoughts, one of which was, *I'd like to shovel this in your mouth!* I wasn't okay, and that was okay. I'm not proud of my ornery thoughts and I was convicted. Humbly, I repented and thanked God for being strong and resilient enough to do the job. Another annoying example was having to pump gas in freezing, bitterly cold weather. It was not only bitter cold outside, but I was very bitter on the inside about the situation. In the end, bitter thoughts will bite you! The fact is, Steve was helpful in very many ways, and I did appreciate that about him.

No matter how small a matter is (pumping gas), God sees and cares about how you feel. He understands the pain behind your reaction, yet greater is the knowledge and experience of how He can personally change your heart from bitterness to acceptance. Ephesians 4:31 commands us to get rid of all bitterness, rage, anger, harsh words, and all those things that can destroy you. The way to remove bitterness is to move toward forgiveness with God's help which can help you break free from the past. The sooner you get over your anger, the better you'll feel. There are literal health benefits in practicing forgiveness—it reduces stress levels, anxiety, and depression, and improves your emotional wellbeing. God specializes in things thought impossible, and He can do what no other one can do. He is the healer of wounded hearts.

> *God specializes in things thought impossible, and He can do what no other one can do.*

Relinquish self-pity and self-reliance; instead, turn your attention and thoughts away from yourself, and become Christ-centered and Christ-focused. The battle begins with a wrong, negative mindset; the battle is won as the mind is renewed. This principle is profound and life-changing. Allow God's Word to fill and renew your mind every day. When your mind is on Christ, Satan has little room to maneuver. Be aware of negative self-talk and gossiping about the one who hurt you.

For a long while, I spent most of my time at my brother Alex's home, my healing place—away from the deafening silence at my home. One afternoon we were target shooting in his backyard. As I held the gun and aimed, a horrible, murderous thought crossed my mind. I actually pictured Steve as the target. I thought how easy it would be to shoot someone who hurt you in the worst possible way. The thought scared me. In that awful mindset, I became painfully aware and remorseful of my sin. I had to confront it and admit how ugly and vitriolic my anger had become. When I admitted the ugly in me and confessed my sin to

Father, He was generous in grace toward me. That breakthrough allowed me to move forward.

In the lonesome and darkest valley, life felt ugly—and I felt ugly. My pet name Ducky didn't seem so cute anymore because rejection made me feel like the Ugly Duckling. Not to mention, this little creature (meaning me) wasn't always silent during the growing pains (more like groaning pains). Thankfully, though, the new and beautiful came into being. God is so patient! It's like Billy Graham said, that the many weeks of silent growth the larva spends in its cocoon are important but there's a moment it "passes through a crisis and emerges a beautiful butterfly. . . . the old and ugly are left behind, and the new and beautiful come into being."[27]

## THE GOOD

It's easy to stand back and wail about the closed door. Yet, there are times when a door will close because that particular one would have caused more harm and unhappiness. With this knowledge, walk forward in grace through those doors that open, and know it is right. Any defeat can be turned into good when you absorb the lesson in it. It's like Romans 8:28 (BSB): "And we know that God works all things together for the good of those who love Him."

## SINGLENESS AND ITS PLUSES

As I write this chapter, I am still single. Thankfully, this season has brought manifold benefits and blessings into my life. What follows is part of an ongoing list as my heart remains open and eager to continue learning and growing with full acceptance of who I am and where I am, just as I am. Writing your own list will boost your spirits, too! Try it and add to the list as time passes because there's joy and contentment in the process.

I seek from singleness . . .

---

27  Billy Graham, *Wisdom for Each Day* (Nashville, TN: Thomas Nelson, 2019).

- Solitude that removes me from clamoring crowds so I can hear my own thoughts.
- Enjoyment of stillness and quiet that calms my soul.
- Wisdom in how I spend time and with whom I choose to spend it.
- To truly understand my desire, purpose, and intention for the possibility of remarriage.
- To guard my heart from the heartless ones whose only goal is to use me to satisfy their lustful cravings.
- To remember my identity comes from the One who created me, gave His life for me, and died for me—Jesus Christ.
- Honesty in recognizing my strengths and weaknesses, positive traits, and character flaws.
- To be content with solitude which can better prepare me for future relationships.
- The ability to distinguish between being lonely and being alone—and avoiding isolation.
- The opportunity to connect with new people.
- The joy and freedom of being me—with all my quirks and idiosyncrasies without any pretense of perfection.
- A greater awareness of others rather than excessive self-focus.
- Faithful friends with integrity who'll be there for me in the good, bad, and ugly, and I, for them.
- Intimacy in friendship without sensuality.
- To be comfortable in my own skin.
- To be aware of self-talk and be kind to myself.
- An unselfish attitude and genuine happiness for those who have found their forever love.
- The humor and good sense to laugh at myself.
- To be patient with myself while working toward a solution to a problem.
- To fully focus on God's purposes of service and ministry.
- Joy in the freedom of making choices and right decisions.

- Less self-absorption and a readiness to encourage others in their journey.
- Complete contentment exhibited through joy, peace, and enduring love.
- To bask in God's love more than ever.
- The opportunity to share with others that God is truly enough.

More than eleven years have passed and much water has gone under the bridge since the separation and divorce. And, oh, how my perspective and attitude have changed for the better! My status is "Single + 1" because I'm never alone. I walk with God. With the passing of time, the pain and hurt of rejection can be numbed, but only God can heal a broken heart. His transforming, amazing, abundant grace, and ineffable love is that which impacts your life and empowers you to forgive what seems unforgivable and love the unlovable. You can be an overcomer, whereby a setback is only a setup for a comeback! Neither striving nor merely surviving, but thriving in joy, peace, and grace; there is *Love Beyond* your status.

# CHAPTER 10

# MIGRATION TO TRANSITION

## *Love Beyond Your Plans*

*"The changes we dread most may contain our salvation."*[28]
—Barbara Kingsolver

**M**igration simply means to go somewhere else. Typically, it's temporary or seasonal like a snowbird (a person who moves to a warmer location when the weather in their area gets cold), and then you come back. That was the plan when Jill Detrick (my girlfriend from Louisville who moved to Arizona) invited me to go on a three-week RV trip. Although it was definitely out of character for this city slicker to go camping (and for three weeks!), it was bound to be an adventure—an allusion to excitement that suited me perfectly! I've often thought if I had refused to go on this RV trip and not stepped out of my comfort

---

28  Barbara Kingsolver, *Small Wonder: Essays* (New York, NY: Harper Perennial, 2003), 13.

zone, my life would've remained the same. My decision to do something different led to a change of life! It's been said that if you want to make God laugh, tell Him your plans. As Proverbs 16:9 puts it—"The heart of man plans his way, but the Lord establishes his steps." You see where I'm going with this, right? Ha!

In July 2019, the saga began when Jill drove Oscar, her reliable and trustworthy RV, across the country from Chandler, Arizona, right to my front door as she managed to maneuver through narrow side streets to my patio home community in Louisville. After loading up my gear, which exceeded the allotted amount, we took off to explore national parks along the route that her son Daniel had previously mapped out. I simply rested. To write about our unprecedented excursion and crazy experiences would take another book! There was a learning curve, but I managed to adapt to the no-privacy zones and live without makeup. I could drive Oscar under very limited conditions, (like a few feet), and according to Jill, I slept "like a dead person," since I don't budge from my position and lie with my hands across my chest. At times, she said she leaned over to see if I was still breathing. For whatever it's worth, it was a ton of fun!

## GOD OF SURPRISES

As planned, at the end of our camping trip, Jill dropped me off in Idaho to visit my son Anthony for a few days before my return to Louisville. However, that plan changed when she invited me to visit her in Arizona—an offer I couldn't refuse. Why not? Flexibility was another key element I learned on the road trip. So, I spread my wings and flew off in a different direction toward Arizona in mid-summer for a short visit with Jill in lieu of returning home.

My short visit extended into a lengthy one. During that time there were interim trips/mini vacations to Santa Fe, New Mexico, and Orlando, Florida, before heading home to Louisville for the Christmas holidays. After each trip, Jill gave me a fresh irresistible invitation to revisit her again, so AZ became my home base. Little did I realize the migration that began in July 2019 would eventually morph into a ten-month odyssey.

In every conceivable way, all my needs were abundantly met. Jill made this possible by giving me a home away from home, completely free, while Daniel, her son, who became my wonderful friend, unselfishly allowed me to use his Sonata Hyundai 24/7 to come and go as I pleased while he was fully recovering from a past injury. (They were, and still are, my extended family.) In November, however, I began wondering and questioning the purpose of this unexplained lengthy vacation. It wasn't because I wanted to leave.

"What's this about?" was the specific question I twice asked God at different junctures of my lengthy stay. It was the vibrant reds and oranges of the autumn season when changes were occurring in nature—and I sensed something was also changing within me. Was there a bigger picture I didn't see or understand? I realized He was providing sufficient time for my wounded heart to continue to heal, ironically, in a desert place! Louisville was where I went through the divorce, and a few years later, it was also where the derailment occurred of a once-hopeful relationship leading to marriage. (Thankfully, it ended.) I realized Father God paved the way for me to leave the "Valley of Baca" (I'll explain this more later) and migrate to a place far away from pain.

*God could decide to move you*
*out of your own way.*

Is something unusual going on in your life that is causing you to question the bigger picture? Maybe you're wondering what purpose it serves. Take your thoughts to the Lord and ask what His plan is to help bring understanding. God could decide to move you out of your own way. It can be one courageous step at a time but trust God in the process, according to Proverbs 16:1 (TPT): "Go ahead and make all the plans you want, but it's the Lord who will ultimately direct your steps."

## UNFORGETTABLE

The following story, which still continues, had a unique beginning—a moment in time that stood still. My girlfriend Carol Howard and I vacationed in 2019 in the small, obscure town of Chimayo, New Mexico. On a cold October afternoon, I met Sonny in a textile shop when "down came the sun." As Carol and I walked in, an employee standing behind the counter immediately caught my eye (actually, both eyes). He was tall, dark, and handsome. It was as if I'd seen this man—in my dreams? Or maybe he *was* the man of my dreams. Either way, it was unsettling, in a good way. We exchanged hellos, he paid a compliment, I thanked him and blushed, and then I browsed through the store.

An interesting conversation soon ensued which began with the usual introductions. My last name, Sandrella, caught his attention—I said he could remember me as "Cinderella." Just barely into the conversation, out of the blue, he said he had a poem to write for me. That spurred me on to share my favorite quote from Shakespeare: "Though she be but little, she is fierce."[29] That further inspired his creative juices. He was a poet, musician (guitarist), and songwriter (and liked to dance!). That was all on my wish list, remember? Our brief encounter led to an easy-going friendly chat that flowed smoothly. Quite enthusiastically, Sonny talked about his grandpa who'd had a great impact on his life, particularly by sharing insight and encouragement regarding the value of time well spent. I noted the fact that Sonny appreciated wisdom and honored his grandpa.

Briefly, I shared a bit of history and insight about my life—I was from Louisville, had a recent break-up, and was now on an extended vacation. But what sent me into a tailspin was a specific question he asked and its

---

29　William Shakespeare, "Though she be but little, she is fierce," *A Midsummer Night's Dream*, Act 3, Scene 2.

wording: "Are you running to or running from?" Sonny read my mail! It was startling! That exact question is what I had been asking God as a heart check-up to be certain my motives and decisions were acceptable to God at this uncertain time of my life. It seemed as though God were speaking directly to me, and Sonny was the conduit. The question wasn't a rebuke but a kind reminder that "all is well," that He and I were running together and was with me even in this remote little town of Chimayo. He even had Sonny here waiting to shake me up a bit. Thankfully, I could confidently answer Sonny, "I'm not running from, I'm running to . . . My heart is running fast toward God!" At times it seemed like I was in a hallway—smack dab in the middle—and I knew I wasn't going back—but neither did I know what was ahead. My final destination? (I mean, other than heaven). And what was the plan? Sonny chuckled because he knew the questions rolling around in my head.

Melissa Helser's song, "I Can't Get Away," perfectly expresses these thoughts. Where could you ever go where God would not be there? Where could you hide? The Lord knows where you are. He knows your heart and your thoughts. You can never outrun His love because He loves you whether you are lost or found. His love surrounds you, and you'll never be able to get away.

Through past experience, I knew I could never outrun pain. No matter how I tried to hide it, bury it, cover it, or run from it, sooner or later, it would overtake me, so I had a frequent "heart check" to stay on the right path.

Sonny was true to his word as he had promised to write a poem that same night and send it to me. You may think I'm fantasizing but it seemed like a love letter from heaven. An ingenious poem, crafted just for me. It touched my heart and is a gift I highly treasure.

With permission granted, I have shared Sonny's poem.

Reflecting on it gave credence to the fact that he intently listened to my story line. Isn't that what God does? This wasn't merely a coincidence but a "God wink." In response, I wrote a poem to Sonny . . . thus beginning a continuing long-distance friendship, encouraging each other in our creative endeavors. In amazement, I still wonder at the impact of that unusual encounter with Sonny, when time stood still, because it's a reminder of the greatness of God's goodness and mercy that follow me all the days of my life.

SHE IS FIERCE

IS SHE RUNNING TO OR RUNNING FROM
WILL SHE GO OR WILL SHE COME
SHE SAID YOU'LL NEVER KNOW ME
BUT HER EYES TELL HER STORY, I CAN SEE

OH, LIKE A BULLET SHE CAN PIERCE
THOUGH SHE BE BUT LITTLE, SHE IS FIERCE
SHE WAS SO FRIGID... SEEMED TO ME
YET IN HER ARMS IS WHERE I WANT TO BE

SHE SAID - IF YOU SEEK IT, YOU WILL FIND
ALL THE BEAUTY AND THE KIND
THAT I CARRY IN MY HEART
ONCE IN MY ARMS... WE'LL NEVER PART

YEA, LIKE AN ARROW SHE CAN PIERCE
THOUGH SHE BE BUT LITTLE, SHE IS FIERCE
SHE IS SO LOVING I CAN SEE
AND IN HER ARMS IS WHERE I WANT TO BE

I ASKED HER WHERE SHE GOING NOW
CAN I GET IN TOUCH WITH HER SOMEHOW
SHE SAID I HAVE NO DESTINY
BUT GOD HAS MADE A PATH FOR ME

AS SHE TURNED AND WALKED AWAY
I HOPED WE'D MEET AGAIN SOMEDAY
IN MY HEART I FELT A PIERCE
THOUGH SHE BE BUT LITTLE, SHE IS FIERCE
YEA....
THOUGH SHE BE BUT LITTLE.......
SHE IS FIERCE

BY Sonny MARTINEZ        To Christina Sandrella

# *It is what it is now but with God, it is not what it always will be.*

Do you feel like a wanderer?

You have a GPS but an unknown destination. Maybe you're questioning your purpose or wondering why you're in such a disappointing situation. God is keenly aware of every detail of your life from beginning to end and vice-versa. He knows exactly where you are geographically and emotionally, exactly how you're feeling with the tumultuous emotions tumbling around in your head. It is what it is now but with God, it is not what it always will be.

He knows your future and when and where you should go, in His perfect timing. Forget about hindsight. You can have foresight. When you listen to God speak and allow Him to lead, then walk in faith until you see by sight. You can "know that for those who love God all things work together for good" (Romans 8:28, ESV). Trust the Father's heart knowing He gives good gifts to His children and has the best for you.

## TRANSITION–TIME TO MOVE

It was February 2020, winter in Arizona, and I sure was enjoying my extended vacay with Jill. However, this unsettling question surfaced again, "What's this about, God?" I was to ascend the mountain. Go higher. Now was the season to move from migration to transition which, ultimately, is the process of change from one form or place to another with no promise of return. To further confirm my move, the pastor of the church, which I was then attending, began a six-week sermon series titled, "Ascend the Mountain." Seriously? Could there've been any clearer confirmation unless Moses had appeared and said, "Go climb the mountain." Months of exploring Arizona and socializing in meetups allowed ample time to become familiar with what would become my new "dwelling place"—although, originally, I never planned to permanently move from Louisville. It just wasn't on my radar. Besides, I had siblings in Louisville and Arizona was a long way from home.

Oftentimes, we won't move unless circumstances force us. The move isn't limited to a geographical destination; it also entails moving forward in decision-making, moving forward in relationships, or reMOVING yourself from unhealthy relationships. You can be assured that God's perfect timetable brings the best results for you because as my friend Toby says, "He does things on purpose for a purpose." And I would add that He does it at the right time. He knows what's ahead.

## A SUITCASE OF MEMORIES

I don't know how I could have come back to the living (after the death of my marriage) had it not been for my children: Randy, Anthony, Mindy, and my siblings, Claudia, Alex, Antoinette, and Jon (and their spouses), who loved me back to life again. We were a close-knit family and their abundance of love, faithful prayers, and continued support helped me combat loneliness. In fact, I practically took up permanent residence with my brother Alex and his wife Cathy. Their secluded, peaceful home in the woods was a haven of rest. And one of their cats was named "Hope," so I went there really often to get hope.

I'm an adventurer but traveling for fun and moving across the country and far away from family are two different matters. It's hard and uncomfortable leaving the familiarity of home, family, and friends, as you appreciate the comfort in the familiar things of life. Patterns of behavior, habits developed over time, and knowing the outcome of certain situations feels good or more secure with fewer risks.

As I prepared to move from Louisville, there was a large accumulation of sentimental mementos over many years that I hadn't the fortitude to separate after the divorce. It was an overwhelming task. But they took action to help absolve that dilemma. At my cry for help, Alex and Cathy, my brother and sister-in-law—came to my rescue for several days and worked assiduously, helping me organize, eliminate, and pack all my stuff. They were not working at the time, but they were worker bees at this job! Alex's laborious task was to pull out items and show them to me, and within five seconds I had to say yes (hold onto) or no (let go). Only a couple of times did I "raise Cain" because I'd had enough! (That means throw a fit.) Poor Alex hung in there with me. Except for the large cumbersome furniture items, Cathy very securely packed everything for the move. They should have been hired and paid! They certainly deserved it. The point is when you're overwhelmed, reach out for help. The attitude of "I can do it myself" is prideful and pointless.

Because I was family-oriented, it was uncharacteristic of me to move away, especially, at such a great distance. So, my family was concerned I might be making a mistake: "Why are you moving to Arizona? Are you sure God is telling you to do so?" The simple and most direct answer was (and still is) "Yes, without a doubt. God's leading me there and making the way for it to happen."

Those who love you most may question your decision the most because they love you. Now, my new friends here ask, "What brought you to Arizona?"

My simple response is, "God did."

It's actually not about the "what" but "who" and "how." Either they understand or they don't. It really doesn't matter.

Although there was no cloud by day or fire by night, God's presence was with me, guiding me. My friend, Jesus, walked with me from the beginning of the new to the end of the old. One of my favorite names for God is Jehovah Shammah, which means "God is already there." He was ahead of me and made the pathway clear to follow. It was time to step into the wilderness, plant myself permanently, and bloom. Of all places, my Promised Land was a desert. Never would I have imagined such a thing. I couldn't help but wonder about the improbability of blooming in a desert (which I formerly thought of as totally barren and desolate).

The destination where God leads you can be somewhat of a mystery. It seems like a big risk, but He knows the right path and the right timing for you to follow. You can count on Him. In the journey, God is developing your trust. In what ways might God be inviting you to move? To make changes? Ask Father to help you remove whatever stands between you and Him. He will do it.

"Trust God from the bottom of your heart; don't try to figure out everything on your own"(Proverbs 3:5, MSG).

## GOD IS ALWAYS ON THE MOVE

Life is a Pilgrimage that doesn't end in this life:

*Blessed are those whose strength is in you,*
*In whose heart are the highways to Zion.*
*As they go through the Valley of Baca*
*They make it a place of springs;*
*The early rain also covers it with pools.*
*They go from strength to strength;*
*Each one appears before God in Zion.*
—*Psalm 84:5-7 (ESV)*

As this journey on the highway to Zion continues, you can thrive and not merely survive. Valleys and mountains, rain and sunshine, all contribute to your growth. Begin, stay, and end with God. He'll not mislead you and He won't abandon you. His name is Emmanuel, "God with us" (you!) and Jesus is WayMaker who goes before you to make a way where there seems to be no way. He makes water gush forth in the wilderness and streams in the desert (see Isaiah 35:6), yet necessary sacrifices are required on any journey, which means giving up something that's valuable or of personal interest. A healthy sacrifice allows you to let go of what's not really best for you, or what doesn't work, in order to embrace what is best and what does work. It's an opportunity that allows you to go from strength to strength.

*A healthy sacrifice allows you to let go of what's not really best for you or what doesn't work in order to embrace what is best and what does work.*

At different intervals of our lives, we're confronted with pain and suffering, yet the Lord Himself comforts and shields us in the places of weeping. The Valley of Baca, mentioned in Psalm 84:6, was an obscure location. Baca means weeping, which can refer to any dark, lonesome valley of despair and loss that we must face and go through. In those times the mantle of God's presence wraps Himself around us, giving us strength and blessing us.

Whether your address changes . . . or your status . . . or your circumstances, open your heart as a welcoming place for God's dwelling so He can guide you. Like Pastor Bill Johnson said, "through life, I realize my true home is found in the presence of God which I carry with me wherever I go." In doing so, you will experience God's *Love Beyond* your own plans and start living your best life.

# CHAPTER 11

# MOUNTAINS

## *Love Beyond the Loftiest Mountain*

*"The mountains are calling, and I must go."[30]*
—JOHN MUIR

**D**o you know what a place is called that you can't get past? It's called a mountain. It's a towering obstacle that appears insurmountable. The thought of mountains creates a plethora of ideas about life and relationships that can feel intimidating or take you to a place of pure enjoyment. It depends on your perception or personal experience. Maybe you've had a fabulous mountain-top euphoric experience! On the other hand, maybe you've encountered a formidable mountain that

---

30 John Muir, "The mountains are calling and I must go," *goodreads,* https://www.goodreads.com/quotes/78007-the-mountains-are-calling-and-i-must-go.

has kept you from moving forward. Seemingly immovable mountains will loom before you on your journey, but you can also scale them.

## THE MOUNTAINS WERE CALLING MY NAME

During the nine months that God was wooing me to Arizona, I sensed Him whispering in my ear—*You are to ascend the mountain.* He's been my Shepherd, and I knew His voice. Since there are plenty of mountains in Arizona, I figured there wasn't a particular one He had in mind (ha!), but I knew there was significance and purpose. There was little to go on, yet my trust in Him was unwavering.

*Faith becomes stronger with each step.*

When it comes to hiking on a mountain, I'm definitely an enthusiast. To ascend simply means to go higher. Oftentimes, God takes you just one step at a time, and that's how I was to climb this mountain. Faith becomes stronger with each step, and to affirm God's mountain message to me, I was reminded of the sermon series "Ascend the Mountain" that was taught at the church I attended. Certainly not a coincidence. God got my full attention. With that word in my head and on my heart, I was on a mission, and mountains became a BIG deal to me!

## GEAR UP AND GET READY

To be successful and avoid unnecessary pitfalls, it's important to make preparations if you're going to climb a mountain. Gear up! There are a few essentials like water, sturdy shoes, and a phone for emergencies (and taking pictures). An extended list could include a first-aid kit, sunscreen, a hat, and hiking poles that keep you steady. Yet, after planning and preparing your best for a mountain hiking adventure, there's still uncertainty as to what lies ahead. This includes a measure of risk and even the possibility of loss. An injury can occur, or a wrong turn can be taken. It's definitely strenuous exercise and presents challenges both mentally and physically. Determination, strength, endurance, grit, and sweat are all part of the process that makes your destination achievable so that you can have success. You then make the decision to "Just do it!"

Likewise, even with much preparation for building a good foundation within a relationship, there's no love without risk or loss. Unexpected challenges still arise that are difficult to navigate. These potential relational hazards include mundane days, boring conversations, monotony, misunderstandings, and feeling neglected or emotionally abandoned when you need your partner the most. Some mornings you wake up next to the man you married and wonder, "What on earth did I do?" Or "What was I thinking?" (Especially before brushing their teeth!). These things happen in the best of relationships. It's like wanting to stay dry when taking a shower—you are going to get wet, all over! There's going to be rough terrain, unknowns, and unpleasant surprises although you prepared as much as possible to face the challenges.

The same principles apply to having a successful relationship. It requires effort, patience, effective and kind communication, unwavering commitment, forgiveness, and I would add consistency. What steps have you taken to become the best partner you can be? Does your life exemplify the traits you want him to have—love, joy, peace, patience, kindness, goodness, and faithfulness? (see Galatians 5:22-23) You and your partner won't be carrying hiking poles, but you will have each other to hold on to and encourage one another when the road gets rocky or a bit slippery.

In relationships, a person can leave and choose another path that will change the course of your life. You feel you've been on track and stayed the course—you've been faithful—yet your relationship has shifted. Perhaps, it ended prematurely and abruptly, which you could never understand. What if God says no to someone you're head over heels for? I've had a few no's from God, and it's not easy when you want a yes! It takes courage to say no or to let go when you long for someone. Take this advice—when you know God says no then go. Pretty simple but breaking up is hard! The sooner the better because you'll find plenty of excuses to stay.

But please never settle for a second because you feel the clock is ticking and love will pass you by. (I'm preaching to myself.) Any decision made from fear will inevitably have its consequences. This is where we must know God's heart—pure love. You might have to break off from a relationship. Just as a wise parent knows when to say no, God our Father withholds some things His children ask for because He IS love and knows what's best. Have you considered there may be circumstances ahead that could hurt or disappoint you greatly, but that God has intercepted your plans by His grace for your protection? He knows everything about you and loves you so much; you can be confident His answer will be best. His no can be a love gift.

However, if you're determined to avoid the messiness of a breakup or inevitable hurts, love will pass you by. In the hope of protecting your heart from being broken, you erect impenetrable walls, and in doing so, you miss the opportunity of being loved and loving others. The truth is that real, honest, genuine love can heal a broken heart.

> *The truth is that real, honest, genuine love can heal a broken heart.*

## EMPTY THE BACKPACK

Remember those "must have" and "must not have" lists I mentioned in chapter six regarding the man I wanted to marry? As time passed, the must-have list got shorter as I got older! Not because I would settle for less or mediocrity, but because I learned what was truly important, valuable, essential, and long-lasting. A godly man who has character! (Not to be confused with a man who IS a character.)

Keep the main thing the main thing. Unrealistic expectations lead to disappointments, so be reasonable about your desires. You can try so hard and expect too much. Lighten the load. Remove from your backpack all non-essentials. Eliminate unnecessary burdens. If it isn't right for you, take the rocks out and keep the gems. What traits do you consider essential in a healthy relationship? Decide three things you must have—uncompromising, nonnegotiable values and beliefs, trust, and commitment—and three things you will not have in a relationship. Write them down, review the list, and update it. Then discard the non-essentials. Empty your backpack of the woe-be-gones—those who are taking up space and time—so you can create more room and have more time for the one who'll not burden you but will lift your burdens. With less weight, you'll enjoy the journey more. My backpack got a lot lighter!

## MOUNTAINS

On the journey, be sure to give rest to your soul along the way because Matthew 11:28 promises that Jesus gives rest to those who are heavy-laden. And while you ascend, say to God, "You are my mountain of strength" (see Psalm 42:9, TPT).

### Ascending

I was reminded of a past hike while visiting my son Anthony in Wyoming. After a day trip to Lander and a good hike up Popo Gai, I wrote the following:

> *Breathing hard on the incline,*
> *For a while, I was sweaty,*
> *But as I climbed higher,*
> *The air was chilly.*

*My nose was wet and runny,*
*But my pace was steady.*
*At the peak of the mountain,*
*The waterfall was frozen.*
*As I scanned mountains so tall,*
*Beholding indescribable beauty and grandeur,*
*I stood there feeling so small,*
*And in amazement and wonder*
*My heart leapt with gratitude*
*To the Creator of it all!*

In the New Testament, mountains are what GIANTS are in the Old Testament, and they have to be removed. You could be facing a giant in your relationship now. Gigantic fear-mongering mountains have names:

Abandonment.

Feelings of unworthiness.

Untrustworthiness.

Lack of confidence.

Lack of trust.

Lies that bring Guilt.

Shame.

And the list goes on. Fear itself is what gives power to the giant, and it can be conquered. If you were standing on a high cliff looking far down upon those giants, you'd get a different perspective. How would they look? As small as ants. Not fierce. Not intimidating. From faith's perspective, you speak to the mountain and tell it to be cast into the depths of the ocean. In other words, move out of my way! Don't let bad news, disappointments, and hurtful situations distort your lens. God is a Mountain Mover working through you to complete your assignment. You've been assigned this mountain to show others that it can be moved.

# *You've been assigned this mountain to show others that it can be moved.*

When you choose to climb the mountain, take on the challenges, and press through the toughest times—the rewards are well worth celebrating! If you stay the course, you will grow stronger. Vulnerability fosters trust, closeness, and intimacy—flexibility allows your partner to feel supported and respected. Practice forgiveness and give grace to free you from harboring bitterness.

Though I can't recall where I read this, Joel Osteen once said:

*When you've made a personal investment in a person or situation, whether it be time, money, or effort, it's easy to feel as though you've been robbed when they walk out or disregard what you've done for them. But we end up robbing ourselves when we stay focused on disappointments because it hinders God from bringing fresh, new blessings into our lives.*

## Climbing the Rough Side of the Mountain

Joel Osteen also says, "Don't quit in the valley; God has a plan for you to reach the mountain top."

The mountain path is neither a smooth, flat, and even road that requires little or no effort, nor is it something you climb carelessly or mindlessly. With uneven hills and inclines, gradual or steep slopes, and sudden changes in altitude or direction, the climb requires awareness and caution. It can rise and fall quickly, making it difficult to navigate. Unexpected potholes trip you up; rocky terrain can cause you to stub your toes. Here in the desert, it takes sharp eyes to avoid thorny cacti such as the prickly pear.

If your life is constrained by the coercive control of a toxic relationship, the Lord will bring you into a new place of wholeness. He is Rescuer and Restorer and will redeem you with an outstretched arm.

Habakkuk 3:19 (NKJV) says "The Lord God [Adonai] is my strength; He will make my feet like deer's *feet*, And He will make me walk on my high heels." He enables you to travel (or hike) difficult terrain with ease so you can scale and stand on the heights. God's purpose is for you to know, experience, and acknowledge His assistance.

### Don't Make a Mountain out of a Molehill

This is easier said than done! Mom was my champion, and often reminded me of this phrase. She was not a worrier but a warrior who practiced what she preached and viewed things from God's perspective. What lens are you looking through? What are you magnifying—the mountain or God? A grandiose mountain in comparison to God's greatness is only a molehill.

> *A grandiose mountain in comparison to God's greatness is only a molehill.*

### Confront and Conquer—Move or Demolish the Mountain

Mountains can't be ignored. They're too prominent—their ominous size looms before you. But visualizing and knowing God's bigness, His mighty power, and sovereignty, gives certainty of victory. God is our Mountain Mover who dwells with us in the realm of possibilities. Speak boldly to the mountain! Tell the mountain how BIG God is. Agree with what Paul says in Romans 8:37: "In all these things we are more than conquerors." God's Word instructs us to speak to that giant standing in our way or causing delay. God can thresh the mountains of opposition and pulverize them!

The Psalmist said, "I will say to God, You are my mountain of strength" (Psalm 42:9, TPT). Your enemy is always on the prowl seeking whom he may devour (see 1 Peter 5:8) and will attempt to pose as another threat on the same mountain—he never stops trying to stand in the way of what God wants for your life. Be aware that he will try to take you around the same mountain again. So, it's important to recognize his schemes, then stand firm and say, "I've already fought and won that battle. You've been defeated!" It is no mistake that Isaiah 54:10 promises: "Though the mountains be shaken, and the hills be removed, yet my unfailing love for you will not be shaken."

But what happens when you pray, and the mountains don't move? It doesn't mean defeat. God gives supernatural ability, overcoming power, and grace sufficient to see you through whatever situation you face, so you can accomplish what He wants you to do. God is WayMaker, and He will make a way. Victory is guaranteed. He will give you the strength to climb the mountain. He will make your feet stable in high places like those of the deer (see Psalm 18:33). Trust and believe while you're in the waiting between the now and not yet. He will mature and help you as He is preparing you for something great! When he says, "Start climbing," in faith, you then move forward and upward, going higher—one step at a time—overcoming obstacles and resolving conflicts. A slow and steady pace is okay. By putting one foot in front of the other, He'll get you where you need to be, and you will come out praising Him on the other side.

*Your perspective changes when a mountain has been conquered. Instead of seeing it as foreboding, it becomes something beautiful.*

Your perspective changes when a mountain has been conquered. Instead of seeing it as foreboding, it becomes something beautiful.

Although the situation hasn't changed, you have a new orientation in your mind. It now represents firmness, constancy, and steadfastness.

I saw the following words on a souvenir magnet from the Grand Teton National Park:

Advice from a Mountain:

Reach for new heights.

Rise above it all.

Rock on.

Savor life's peak experiences.

Be uplifting.

Just as Moses answered the call of God to come up higher, to ascend the mountain of Sinai so he could encounter God in a way he never had before, we are also called to come up higher. Draw near to God and He'll draw near to you (see James 4:8). The good news is you don't have to climb a physical mountain. You have been called to ascend a spiritual mountain called Mt. Zion which represents the abiding presence of God in your life. As you climb, love will carry you and lift you up almost effortlessly when you are weak. Free fall into the loving arms of Jesus!

*Love Beyond* the loftiest mountain.

# CHAPTER 12

# LET LOVE LIFT YOU HIGHER

## *Love Beyond Yourself*

*"If you would be loved, be lovable."*[31]
—OVID

L ord, I recognize an implacable passion within my soul, calling me onwards and upwards to You. With eyes fixed upon You, and my heart set upon this pilgrimage, I choose to walk on Your life paths so I can experience Your plans for my life.

What does love **look** like to you? What does love *feel* like to you? Out of curiosity, I asked a few friends these two questions. Below are their comments.

---

31 Ovid, "If you would be loved, be lovable," *goodreads,* https://www.goodreads.com/quotes/209577-if-you-would-be-loved-be-lovable,

## WHAT LOVE LOOKS LIKE

*He will want to know who I am to connect with my heart because he doesn't just want my body.*

*He doesn't give up pursuing me even when I'm at my worst.*

*Love is thoughtfulness.*

*He's there for me when I need his help.*

*He takes time for me.*

*Love is warm hugs that say, "I love you."*

*Love creates happy memories.*

*It looks like laughter and sharing food around the dinner table.*

*It's radiant and pure—no strings attached or manipulation.*

*It is kind and thoughtful and likes to please me.*

*It's a foot massage.*

*It's an admiring smile.*

*It's the quality of being friendly and considerate.*

*Love is when there's a batch of cookies, and he gives me the last one!*

*Love is day trips and exploring new places.*

*He likes to make me smile.*

*He brings me flowers for no special occasion but "just because."*

*He is generous—not just with money—but with sincere compliments.*

*He is a gentleman and opens my car door.*

*Love is romantic—slow dancing and writing me poems.*

*Love appreciates my opinions and understands my desires.*

*Knowing him helps me become a better person.*

*It is hiking, sweating, and breathing hard!*

## WHAT LOVE FEELS LIKE

*It is enjoyable.*

*It feels like contentment.*

*Love is quiet moments—without having to fill the gap of silence with incessant small talk.*

*It feels wonderful when he looks at me and listens intently like he's reading me.*

*He is affectionate when he smiles at me and soothing when he strokes my hand.*

*It only feels like true love when he really wants to know ME—who I am.*

*It's feeling special—not awkward but comfortable.*

*It feels warm and blissful, cozy, easy, and peaceful.*

*It's freedom to be me without having to be perfect!*

*Love is a sense of trustworthiness—I can talk to him about anything without feeling judged.*

*It's a partnership. Mutual respect.*

*I feel cared for because he wants to help me—no pressure!*

*It feels gentle and secure.*

*It's wild when he takes my breath away by the way he looks at me!*

*I would never want to live without him.*

*It's a warm feeling in my chest—the saying to "warm the cookies of my heart" comes to mind; it's felicity—intense happiness and joy.*

*It will feel like my heart is dancing.*

I sensed deep emotion in their expression and appreciated their honest, transparent answers. Notice there were no huge demands! Every desire is reasonable, achievable, and worthy of respect.

As previously mentioned, according to Google reports, romance is the most popular book genre. Despite the high interest in romance, there are alarming statistics in the most intimate of relationships—marriage.

Almost 50 percent of all marriages in the US will end in divorce or separation.

Sixty percent of second marriages end in divorce.

Seventy-three percent of all third marriages end in divorce.

Living together (cohabitating) prior to marriage can increase the chance of getting divorced by as much as 40 percent.

Pornography addiction was cited as a factor in 56 percent of divorces.

Obviously, reading about love isn't the answer.

## WHAT LOVE IS NOT

It isn't being absorbed with self. Self-focused love becomes distorted—what can you do for me? Or, look how great I am! What if it's not actually about you? For example: self-esteem, self-reliance, self-image, self-confidence, self-consciousness, etc. There's much talk about self-love which ultimately puts "self" before God. I understand we must love ourselves in order to love others. The very essence of love is God. Should we not get our value from Him and believe what He says about us? Should we not rely on Him instead of ourselves? And reflect His image? Confidence is found in knowing our identity in Christ, not finding it within; should we be more conscious of ourselves, or have less of us and more of Him? Love is not SELFISH. He will take you so much higher than you can take yourSELF.

One very popular song in the mid-60s was "You've Lost That Lovin' Feelin'." In this iconic hit, the Righteous Brothers sang about how their lover's touch lacked tenderness. She didn't close her eyes anymore when they kissed, and her eyes no longer communicated welcome when they reached for her. The lesson is obvious—once you start criticizing everything your spouse does, that which had been precious and beautiful will die.

As wonderful as those feelings of "love" are, if a feelin' is all there is, we are all at a loss. Butterflies and chills up and down the spine are exciting, but they are fickle, too. When that feeling is gone, or the cycle dies down, what then? People say many things:

"We grew apart and fell out of love."

"I wasn't happy anymore."

"We became two different people."

People are divorcing because they lost that feeling. But what they have truly lost is their commitment (if they ever had one). Commitment means staying loyal to what you said you would do long after the mood you said it in has left you. Otherwise, what remains are only unfulfilled promises and vain hope.

*Commitment means staying loyal to what you said you would do long after the mood you said it in has left you.*

A few years after my divorce, I was very much in love with someone, and we were planning to marry. So, I posed this question: "Can you guarantee you'll never leave me? Never divorce me?" He was stunned, faltering, at a loss for words, but I tried to ignore his obvious discomfort as he stumbled upon a few words.

"Well, no. How can I predict the future? I don't know what's ahead . . ."

Ultimately, if I no longer "made him happy" and he wanted to leave me, he would find an EXIT door. Obviously, there was no wedding.

There's never an assurance of what tomorrow holds. How does that influence one's decision not to have a forever marriage? What keeps a couple together is the treasure that's kept in their heart—a commitment. Be vulnerable enough to talk honestly about your differences and how you're feeling.

I cringe at some excuses for a divorce: "I'm just not the same person as when I got married. I've changed." I sure hope you're not the same person—I hope you're a better person. Change is inevitable. Your body changes, as does your hairline!

"I'm not happy in the marriage." Poor, selfish you.

"We no longer have anything in common." And who's to blame?

Please understand that I'm aware of situations where divorce is necessary if your life is in danger. But if people would take their marriage more seriously, divorce would be less likely. Perhaps, your perspective has changed on certain subjects, even goals and ideas could be different. What should remain intact are values and beliefs, those principles that contribute to your personhood. Take positive action and stay connected! Communicate instead of looking to see if the grass is greener on the other side. Take the effort to dig into the serious issues and seek counsel when necessary. Every day, be intentional by putting time and effort into the relationship with the bodacious commitment of growing together and staying together. Keep the fires burning! God is love. Put Him at the center of your relationship.

The apostle Paul said that REAL love is:

> *Large and incredibly patient. Love is gentle and consistently kind to all. It refuses to be jealous when blessing comes to someone else. Love does not brag about one's achievements nor inflate its own importance. Love does not traffic in shame and disrespect, nor selfishly seek its own honor. Love is not easily irritated or quick to take offense. Love joyfully celebrates honesty and finds no delight in what is wrong. Love is a safe place of shelter, for it never stops believing the best for others. Love never takes failure as defeat, for it never gives up. Love never stops loving.* —1 Corinthians 13:4-8 (TPT)

Put this to the test every day by practicing it. Take an honest assessment daily of these attributes and ask: What have I done well? What should I improve upon? Have I actively demonstrated love today? By examining ourselves according to this description of love, would there not be more growth, joy, achievement, and excellence in loving others?

As I was writing, a past Facebook post from May 17th, 2019, popped up on my wall. It's amazing how its message coincides perfectly with this chapter.

> *Real love is often hard, inconvenient, and costly; but true happiness only comes to those who care about others at some cost to themselves. Why, then, does it get so twisted and so far removed from the real thing? I believe it's because either the scriptures from 1 Corinthians 13:4-8 are ignored, or people are ignorant of them. Love makes sacrifices! And I'm not talking about being a martyr. Yet, in the midst of hurt and all the other negative emotions, there is a sense of peace in knowing*

*the grace and love of Jesus that enables and equips me to go beyond self-love.*

## LOVE THE UNLOVABLE

Every human being deserves to be loved—even scoundrels and the worst sinner. (You might want to re-read that to let it sink in!) Our intellect resists such a preposterous idea, especially if you have personally suffered harm and have a wounded heart; yet the life of Jesus is evidence of loving the unlovable and extending forgiveness. (I know some scoundrels—how about you?)

*Every human being deserves to be loved— even scoundrels and the worst sinner.*

## LOVE DOES–TURN YOURSELF INSIDE OUT

Some things you can't change. Other times things change you.

GIVE LOVE when you feel the least loved and need it the most.

SMILE when greeting someone even if it hurts or feels awkward.

BE HAPPY for the couples and families you see who are having a good time.

ENJOY THE COMPANY OF A FRIEND although you'd rather have that special someone in your life.

JOIN A MEETUP OR FACEBOOK GROUP instead of isolating yourself.

WATCH YOUR WORDS and avoid "hate talk" about yourself or criticizing your former spouse or boyfriend.

LISTEN TO HAPPY MUSIC and dance like nobody's watching.

FIND A BIBLE BELIEVING CHURCH and get connected in community.

## FINDING YOUR *WHY*

Your "why" is a motivating factor that keeps you moving forward when the going gets really tough, particularly in marriage.

### Why I Got Married

At the age of nineteen, I knew I wanted to spend the rest of my life with Steve. I wanted his companionship and love forever and I wanted to reciprocate it.

I wanted to have children, to have our family, and create lifelong memories.

I wanted us to serve God together, pray together, and fulfill God's purpose for us as a couple. I operated according to two fundamental beliefs for Christian marriages: they will last forever, and the spouses will be faithful.

## THE SKY IS THE LIMIT!

Soon after my divorce, I had quite an awesome adventure—tandem skydiving! I jumped with an instructor, and my son Randy, who is an enthusiast, agreed to go, too. (He didn't need convincing.) It was deemed my "Freedom Flight" and, frankly, I couldn't have been more scared!

With Steve being a pilot, my decision to jump out of a plane was a mental reenactment of being set free. Yeah, a divorce can make you do crazy things. It wasn't a celebration of the divorce—I was grieving—but gliding down to earth with a parachute sure allowed me to see things from a different perspective. Besides that, Randy and I have an unforgettable memory and image of that incredible experience together. (His wife, Jenna, had her doubts!)

When you're hurting, do something crazy (not stupid!) or, at least, unusual or different. It doesn't have to be spectacular but help yourself get out of the funk and have someone participate with you that you love. Don't do it alone. Create a wonderful, unique memory! This brings to mind another adventure—hot air ballooning...

## HOT AIR BALLOONING

### Soaring in the Wind Stream of Holy Spirit

This experience actually occurred when I was married and took place in New Zealand. It is a good analogy for relationships. Hot air balloons work because hot air rises. A burner heats the air inside the balloon (the controlled fire was amazing!) and with the air cooler on the outside, the balloon begins to float upwards. By controlling the temperature of the air inside the balloon, it begins to descend and eventually land.

What did I learn? People need to "flame a fire of passion" in their relationships that produces heat and flickers and dances. Be passionate in loving each other and wanting to please the other. Balloons travel in the direction of the wind. How are the winds of life affecting you? Rick Warren describes four different kinds of wind: change, opposition, temptation, and conflict. Don't settle for staying grounded when you're meant to soar! Keep the fire burning!

## LOVE HAS A NAME

First John 4:8, in every English version of the Bible, states the following: "God is love." Love has a name: God. Love is the very essence of creation and the defining characteristic of His presence. God is relational, a Father, passionate and caring, loving people and desiring companionship. Your insatiable longing for love is because you were created in God's image to have a heart connection with Him. God is in pursuit of you! As in any true relationship, there can only be fulfillment if the pursuit goes both ways. "Neither height nor depth, nor anything else in all creation, will be able to separate me from the love of God that is in Christ Jesus my Lord" (Romans 8:39, NIV).

## *The greatest investment in someone's life is love.*

The greatest investment in someone's life is love.

Freely receive! Freely give! Love is finding a place of need and meeting that need. The Golden Rule, found in Matthew 7:12 (NIV), still rules! "Do to others what you would have them do to you." Sometimes the simplest gesture of kindness opens doors to hearts. Extend yourself, and reach out to others, so they can taste and see how good God is (see Psalm 34:8). Carry J-O-Y to someone: Jesus—Others—You. It can be found in some of the least expected places and uncovered in unlikely people: a cashier at the grocery, a salesperson, a server in a restaurant, your neighbor, the stranger sitting next to you in church, or someone walking in the park.

Seize every opportunity. Your life is to be as a free-flowing river that gives fresh water to those who are thirsting for love. Love has no strings attached. Give gladly and plenteously with no expectation of something in return. Hopefully, it will become contagious and spread wildly through others. Love much while in the waiting for the special one! Pass love on!

## FIRST THINGS FIRST

If you knew you had only a few minutes left on earth, what would your most important priorities be? Most likely, you'd call out to God and then tell the people in your life that you love them. Life is about relationship with God and the people you love. In Matthew 22:35-40, Jesus said we are to love the Lord our God with all our heart, with all our soul, and all our mind, and our strength. Our entire being! Then He urged us to love our neighbor as ourself. He also told us exactly how to do that:

"Let me tell you why you are here. You're here to be salt-seasoning that brings out the God-flavors of this earth. . . . You're here to be light, bringing out the God-colors in the world" (Matthew 5:13-14, MSG).

I don't yet see him, but I hold on to the promise that I'll have someone to hold onto. That my knight in God's shining armor is on his way!

Meanwhile, there's a place of snug contentment just for me in the arms of Jesus. I adore Him, and He adores me. He's around to stay, and He never quits on me. If you have not received Jesus into your life, He stands at the door of your heart and knocks. Love has found you! Invite Him in, become a beneficiary of His lavish love, and be a source of grace and blessing to others that supersedes all you've ever known (see Ephesians 3:20). Love will take you higher than you've ever been.

*Each day, as you passionately pursue God, you're on a mission to Love Beyond yourself.*

Song of Solomon 2:10 (NIV) says, "My beloved spoke and said to me, 'Arise, my darling, my beautiful one, come with me.'" Keep close to Jesus every day all day. Morning, noon and night. Each day, as you passionately pursue God, you're on a mission to *Love Beyond* yourself and reach out to others who need love.

"Belovedness" is a song by Sarah Kroger that tells how you've owned fear and self-loathing, voices inside your head that say you're a failure; now it's time to own your belovedness. You let your past define you and what everybody else says, now it's time to hear what your Father says and own your belovedness. He finds you beautiful and His love is fierce. Whatever it takes, He'll find you. Lies said you weren't enough, but you are completely loved, and His heart is your home. It's time to own your belovedness. . . .

Beloved, it's time to come home.

9 781960 678164